SD

D0319746

FREDDIE FLINTOFF

ENGLAND'S HERO

A NOTE FROM THE AUTHOR...

Thank you to Cherry and Anthony Aldred, Greg Baum, Tim de Lisle, Emma John, Kate Laven, the Reverend Malcolm Lorimer and his amazing file of cuttings, Steven Lynch, Osman Samiuddin, John Stern, Sharda Ugra, and Joy and Ian Wilson for their great child-minding and restaurant service. To Andy and Rosy for being lovely and to my baby nephew, Freddie Liam, born into a world where England hold the Ashes and a Lancastrian is the best all-rounder in the world.

REFERENCES

Cricinfo; *Guardian Unlimited*; *All Out Cricket*; *Wisden Cricket Monthly*; *The Wisden Cricketer*; *The Lancashire Cricket Yearbook*; *Wisden Cricketers' Almanack*; *The Lancashire Evening Post*; *The Manchester Evening News*; *The Guardian*; *The Independent*; *The Mirror*; *The Sun*; *The Daily Telegraph*; *The Times*; *The Independent on Sunday*; *The News of The World*; *The Observer*; *The Melbourne Age*; *The Sydney Morning Herald*; Channel 4's cricket coverage.
Being Freddie: My Story So Far by Andrew Flintoff, Hodder and Stoughton, 2005
Freddie: The Biography of Andrew Flintoff by Tim Ewbank, John Blake Publishing, 2005
My Life in Pictures by Andrew Flintoff with Patrick Murphy, Orion, 2004.

First published in 2005

© Carlton Books 2005

All rights reserved. No part of this publication may be reproduced, stored in a retrieval system, or transmitted in any form or by any means, electronic, mechanical, photocopying, recording or otherwise, without the prior permission of the copyright owner and publishers.

A CIP catalogue record for this book is available from the British Library

ISBN 1 84442 216 X

Words Tanya Aldred
Editor Justyn Barnes at Justyn Barnes Media Ltd
Art Director Paul Sinclair at Parallax Studios
Cover design Darren Jordan
Commissioning Editor Martin Corteel
Photography Empics, Rex Features, *Manchester Evening News*

Printed in United Kingdom

FREDDIE FLINTOFF
ENGLAND'S HERO

TANYA ALDRED

3/06

0043722873

796.358092

CARLTON
BOOKS

CONTENTS

INTRODUCTION

Summer 2005: the Australian cricket team came to England certain that they would retain the Ashes urn that they had held firmly for 18 years. This notion was destroyed by a vibrant, young England team, inspired by all-rounder Andrew "Freddie" Flintoff. In a series that even seized the imagination of those with just a passing interest in cricket, no-one epitomized the competitive fire and sportsmanship of the two teams more than Flintoff. This is the story of an ordinary Preston lad who became England's hero...

the new

KING

of England

A weary, beery man stood at the front of the open-top bus. His eyes were hidden behind wraparound shades, his tie was askew, but his mouth was smiling. In one arm he held his one-year-old daughter Holly and, in the other, a bottle of beer. He took a swig and then saluted the crowd; a very tired, rather drunk man mountain. And the crowd saluted him back – 100,000 of them in total, 25,000 in Trafalgar Square alone. "Super Fred," they chanted, "Super Fred." Over and over again.

It had been a long, undulating haul to the top for Andrew Flintoff. He had been hailed too early, overwhelmed with promises and seduced by other pleasures. "I got a little lost in it all – the cars, the houses and the drinking. I'd lost sight of what I was trying to do," he admitted. "Now I just concentrate on my cricket."

But even this Ashes year, the path had been rocky. In January, he had an ankle operation and spent months training to get back to full fitness. Then his first Ashes Test arrived, at Lord's, only for England to be trounced. He went to Devon with his family to rethink and, on his return, was transformed into Super Fred. He dominated the rest of the series, scoring his first Ashes century, grabbing his second five-wicket haul in Tests, finishing top of the England bowling averages and near the top of the batting, but the figures disguised the whole story. His huge hands had pummelled the Tests this way and that, in an unbelievable sequel of too-close-to-call matches that ended at last with that victory at The Oval in the final hours of the last day of the series. He finished it a cricketing colossus.

So, that Tuesday morning, Flintoff was the undisputed King of England, with Kevin Pietersen his lusty Prince of Wales, as the bus parade crawled from the Lord Mayor's house to Nelson's column, the day after England won back the Ashes for the first time in nearly 19 years.

It had been a long summer, a long series, a long match, and a long, long night. The beers were opened when England were declared winners in the September evening sun. They continued to be opened during an Anglo-Australian dressing-room booze-up, then back at the Grange City Hotel near Tower Bridge, then again at the Soho nightclub Kabaret Prophecy and, lastly, back at the hotel.

There, at quarter to six in the morning, a BBC radio reporter found Flintoff looking amiably off his trolley with a gin and tonic in his hand. At a quarter to eight it was a vodka and cranberry; a bit later, with a friendly morning beer in his hand, he gave an informal interview. "I'd never make a decent celebrity," he said. "I'm ugly, I'm overweight but I'm happy." His manager Neil Fairbrother then ordered him upstairs to his bedroom to take a shower and change his clothes for the victory parade.

Somehow, Flintoff managed to make it onto the England victory bus. Mike Gatting – the last Ashes-winning captain – asked if he had eaten anything. "Yeah, a cigar," Gatting was told, as another glass of champagne was pushed into Flintoff's hand.

"I did briefly wonder what state he would be in," England's left-arm spinner Ashley Giles admitted later. "But, as always, he was very mellow and very relaxed. If he has a drink, I have never known him to get in anyone's face."

Many had blanched when it was announced that the ECB had booked Trafalgar Square for a victory parade before the Oval Test had even started. But their confidence had not been misplaced. It had been a long time since anyone could say that about the England cricket team.

**Chapter opener: Champagne moments as Freddie celebrates winning the 2005 Ashes.
Right: Flintoff was the dominant figure in the best Ashes series ever.**

By the time the bus arrived in Trafalgar Square – preceded by police horses and motor cycles, and followed by another bus carrying the England women's team who had also won their Ashes series and had been invited to share the acclaim coming down from roof-tops, out of office windows, and up from the thousands lining the streets – Flintoff was waning. "To be honest, David, I'm struggling," he told David Gower, a member of the last England side to have won an Ashes series in England, who was attempting to interview him on a podium. "I've not been to bed yet, the eyes behind these glasses tell a thousand stories."

"It's been a roller-coaster. We played against a great Australian side who are full of world-class performers, but every time a performance was needed one of us stood up and delivered it."

Inhibitions flushed away, he then gave the organizers of the forthcoming Super Series in Australia – in which he would play for the World XI – an unexpected plug. "I've got the Super Series in two weeks' time – I can't think of anything worse." Encouraged, he grabbed the microphone and attempted to serenade the crowd with the Flintoff version of "Suspicious Minds", one of his favourite Elvis classics, before the sound system magically seemed to disconnect. The sun beat down and the atmosphere grew more surreal as everyone joined in with a chorus of "Jerusalem" – the anthem of the summer – and a selection of Barmy Army classics.

"It's a surreal moment, because I don't think cricket's ever reached these heights of celebration," the captain Michael Vaughan said over the whirring sound of police and media helicopters.

There were even Australians in the crowd, despite having had the famous urn stolen from them. Australian Foreign Minister Alexander Downer, in London at the time, was not one of them. He sent his congratulations, but that was as far as it went. "We understand only too well the great excitement there is in London with England winning the Ashes," he said. "For us, we drive past the celebrations as fast as our car will go."

From Trafalgar Square, the players were taken to Downing Street where the Prime Minister Tony Blair – not a renowned cricket fan – held a reception in their honour. Alcohol was not a guest, until someone hinted that it might come in useful and some white wine was opened. "It was a bit warm but you can't have everything I suppose," sighed the Yorkshire swing bowler Matthew Hoggard. It was a surreal sight, with the huge Geordie fast bowler Steve Harmison sitting on a swing belonging to one of the Blair children because there weren't enough benches; Pietersen was having a long chat with the Prime Minister's wife Cherie, before asking, after saying a fulsome goodbye, who she was; and Flintoff wandering around in a haze – he later admitted that he didn't think that he had met the PM, because he'd been so interested in having a look around the Cabinet room.

From one HQ to another – it was back to Lord's for the final reception and awards. For some, there was another night of celebration ahead, but Flintoff had had enough.

He arrived back at the hotel with a blue moustache and messages scrawled over his forehead with biro – Harmison later admitted that he had been the culprit – and slept that night the sleep of a very, very hungover man.

As did many others from Preston to Penzanze, such was the joy in beating Australia, something many had given up seeing again in their lifetime, satisfying their longing instead by sighing over thumb-eared images of a tubby Gatting celebrating just before the turn of the year in 1986.

Gatting's chief weapon then was a 31-year-old all-rounder by the name of Ian Botham; Michael Vaughan's main weapon, a 27-year-old called Andrew Flintoff. The comparisons, with which Flintoff had been saddled since he was only just out of his teens and a raw talent with a tendency to self-destruct, at last reflected a truth, of sorts.

They are two very different sorts of men, with different talents and hugely different personalities. But each are possessed with the same power to change a game with an unplayable ball, a brilliant catch or a murderous stroke, that could in turn inspire team-mates to play beyond their powers.

"He's got so many Botham traits. That 'here, give

**Previous pages: "Tired and "emotional" in Downing Street with team–mate Kevin Pietersen.
Right: One hundred thousand people came out to glimpse England's Ashes victory bus parade.**

me the ball, I'll do it' attitude," said David Lloyd, Flintoff's coach first at Lancashire and then with England. "He's an inspiration to the players around him and those watching. He's got a Bothamesque response from spectators because he never gets above himself.

"Andrew's a people's player. He's always got time for those who care about the sport and he's never been any different. I believe that character, and how he conducts himself, comes from his parents and his upbringing."

The heady days went on. The Queen sent a telegram and the Prime Minister issued a statement. It was announced that the England team were to be immortalized philatelically – the Royal Mail would release a set of stamps in their honour. Flintoff himself was rumoured to be doing an array of the bizarre and impossible: an appearance in a Flintstones movie, a cameo role in the Channel 4 hit programme *Shameless*, releasing a Christmas single and starring in a 2005 calendar expected to out-sell David Beckham's. Back in the real world, he was given the freedom of Preston.

"Andrew Flintoff may be an international superstar these days, but he is Preston born and bred and has always remained proud of his roots," said the Mayor. "He is a great role model and epitomises everything we want to portray Preston as – young, vibrant, enthusiastic and going places."

"That means I can drive a flock of sheep through the town centre, drink for free in no less than 64 pubs and get a lift home with the police when I get inebriated – what more could you want?" the new Freeman mused happily.

But Flintoff wasn't much interested in the new celebrity life that was opening up before him. On the Friday night after the Ashes, he was found not in a sweaty London club but at a little cricket club in Marple, near Manchester, supporting the benefit of Lancashire's second-team captain Gary Yates.

In Australia, the truth was slowly dawning – the Ashes were not coming back. A few long-suffering exiled England supporters organized an open-top bus parade through central Sydney to ram home the message, past the house of cricket-loving Prime Minister John Howard, flying giant St George's flags and waving replica urns.

And the man chiefly responsible, Flintoff, seemed to have come from nowhere. "Flintoff had no profile in Australia before this Ashes series," explained Greg Baum of *The Melbourne Age*. "That made his exploits even more astonishing here. Previously, he was known only in the abstract, as an archetypal England player of the day, the next big thing who never arrived. He was always injured, always fat, always had an excuse. He had never played against Australia in a Test match, and forgettably in three one-day internationals.

"It would be fair to say, then, that Flintoff held no fears. So this demonic all-rounder who came to dominate the series came not just as a revelation, but a shock. That lusty hitting; no-one had done that to us for years (apart from Pietersen, who we couldn't take very seriously). That mesmerizing swing bowling; we hadn't seen anything like it since Damien Fleming's last injury. That heart: 18 overs in a row when the pressure was really on. This was the antithesis of everything that we had become conditioned to believe about an England cricketer. This was not another Hollioake, after all, but truly the next Botham.

"But the really disconcerting thing was that although he was a hero to England, he could not be an anti-hero in Australia. He was too likeable for that. He roared like Maximus after taking a wicket, but observed all the niceties, going first to console Brett Lee when the epic of Edgbaston was at last finished before he was swept up by euphoric team-mates. Suddenly, even the Australians were saying 'well bowled' and 'after you'. Flintoff was changing both the face of cricket and its heart."

His life was also changing. On the way back from London, he had been sitting in the train with the co-writer of his autobiography, trying to bang out the last chapter in time to catch post-Ashes fever. He had been warned that a gaggle of photographers awaited him at Manchester Piccadilly station so he got off a stop early at Stockport and drove home. But there were photographers there, too. Things would never be the same again.

Left: Legendary all-rounder Ian Botham with the man who has now assumed a similarly lofty status in world cricket.

the scrawny boy with

potential

It is summer, some time in the late 1980s, and the Flintoff brothers have gone to Blackpool. Christopher, the older by three-and-a-half years, has gone to watch Lancashire play at Stanley Park. Down by the windy seafront is his younger brother Andrew, a beanpole of a curly blond-haired boy, who has chosen instead to play on the slides at Professor Peabody's in the town's famous Tower. He's having a whale of a time. But cricket would not be kept waiting much longer.

Andrew Flintoff was born at the Royal Preston Hospital on 6 December 1977. His father Colin worked for British Aerospace as a maintenance man and his mother Susan did a variety of jobs including teaching at a reception class nearby.

The Flintoffs lived in a house on Lauderdale Road in the middle of Preston – an old Lancashire mill town on the banks of the River Ribble, an important centre of the cotton industry during the Industrial Revolution but by then becoming a centre of engineering.

Cricket coursed through the family veins. Colin played local league cricket at Dutton Forshaw, which soon became a second home for his sons. Andrew, who was promenaded around the boundary ropes in his pram and sat happily astride the mowing machine with his dad, played his first game as a six year old, wearing his Manchester United tracksuit. Not long afterwards he was playing senior cricket and, for a time, he was in the same team as his dad and his brother. A friend remembers an autumn day when the returning primary school children had to write what they did in the holidays. Andrew wrote a fantasy of runs and wickets. The supply teacher wrote "what a dream"; the other children told her it was true.

Andrew Flintoff had inherited his father's huge platters of hands and his Dad could see that Andrew had talent. One day he saw an advertisement on the back of the *Lancashire County Cricket Handbook*. It mentioned a Lancashire schools Under-11 side. Colin phoned up, took Andrew along and soon the scouts spotted some raw talent. He was in the system. Later that year, aged nine, he had already played a few games.

He remembers his first game, against Derbyshire Under-11s. He was 12th man. "There was a girl playing for the other side, I remember it was raining and the ground was just off the A50 where the big chimneys are. I fielded for about ten overs, I was over the moon just getting on." He was hooked, and when he was given his first Lancashire Under-11 cap he was so chuffed that he wore it for a week. He made his first hundred against Kent at the Dartford Festival – still one of his proudest cricket moments – and was soon playing alongside Phil Neville, later of Manchester United and England. Neville was probably the better cricketer, but football was his first love and he was lured to the more lucrative Old Trafford just over the road.

John Wylie, who was in charge of the Lancashire Under-11 team, told *The Daily Telegraph*: "He has a remarkable eye, but had to learn to play straight because as a nine-year-old, he needed that to survive against older lads.

"Even at a young age he was a magnificent fielder and took catches no-one else could. Against London Schools aged 11 he thrashed the attack around the ground – and that included Alex Tudor. By the time he was 11, his third year in the team, he led the side to an unbeaten season, with 1,000 runs and 50 wickets."

To start with there was time to squeeze in a few other interests: a spot of football, the odd bit of table tennis, then there was chess. He played for the county side, and years later beat a rather perturbed Mike Atherton on a jolting bus during a Lancashire pre-season tour of Jamaica. There were a few games of mini-rugby – Preston Grasshoppers were interested – but by then cricket was calling loud and clear. Flintoff just loved it, loved watching bang-crack players like Ian Botham and Viv Richards, loved the feeling of the bat in his hands. By the time he was 13 he had moved clubs to St Anne's, near Blackpool, for a higher standard of opposition and started playing with professionals.

He was tall but had a scrawny build – he used to wear T-shirts under his cricket shirts to make him look bigger – and he was shy with strangers. He arrived for his debut for the Fourth XI, with his head down. Asked to open the innings by a curious captain, and with only a cap on his head, he thrashed around a burly Scottish fast bowler, to score 32 of the 47 runs needed. After a quick glass of squash he was off home again, leaving some reeling team-mates and an ego-squelched Scot. Only a year or so later he knocked up a cosy 232 in a 20-over game for St Anne's Under-15s. It is still his highest score.

At 14, he was the youngest player to be selected for the First XI and was soon building a reputation for himself – cracking the tiles, breaking windows and landing the ball on the breakfast table of the houses behind the sightscreen at one end of the ground. The club received fired-up phone calls from their peppered neighbours and were forced to up their insurance premiums. John Cotton, the chairman of St Anne's, said: "If anyone was going to make it as a cricketer, it was him. He didn't realize his own strength. He could throw the ball the length of the ground."

Then came the lucky break. At just 15 years old he was called up to make his debut for the Lancashire Second XI against Glamorgan. "Dad was chuffed to bits but I was bricking it to be honest," he said. He did nothing spectacular, making 26 and 13, but it was the beginning of his career proper. And it was from the second-team coach John Stanworth that he got his popular moniker, "Freddie" – purely

because Flintoff sounded so like Flintstone (now, only his parents and wife call him Andrew).

All this might have impressed spectators on cricket grounds, but they just weren't interested at Ribbleton Hall High. "No-one was bothered," says Flintoff. "I went to quite a rough school in Preston and we played football all year round – cricket wasn't too popular because it was a posh game. I had to play football as well for the school to save face. It was football, summer and winter. Just keep your head down." On a careers form he wrote "professional cricket" and was told to think again.

"I never thought about being a pro until I started playing for the second team at Lancs in the fourth year, and school went downhill when it looked as if Lancashire were going to give me a contract. I still got my GCSEs, but probably not as well as I should have done."

His back was to be the bane of his early cricketing life. He had periods, often years, without bowling; scans and counter scans and diagnoses of this and that. He was told that when his body caught up with its own growth spurt, he would be okay, but he often doubted whether he would be able to make it as an all-rounder. He probably wasn't helped by coaches from England schools mucking about with his front-on bowling action and producing a hybrid which did nothing for his anatomy.

He left school at 16, with nine GCSEs, though his mum and dad were keen for him to carry on with his education. King Edward's School, Lytham, had offered him a sixth-form scholarship because of his cricket, and Northamptonshire had tried to wheedle him out of Lancashire's clutches with the promise of a place at Oundle School. But Flintoff was now dreaming in red roses.

His mum however was no pushover. Not keen on having a lounging Flintoff sloping around the house, she packed him off to find a job. He was soon behind the record counter at Woolworths where he developed an obsession with Elvis. A greatest hits compilation had just come out and, within a couple of weeks, his scorn turned to enjoyment. Within a month he knew all the words.

Life was changing in other ways, too. "My school

friends drifted away to be honest – in the evenings I went to play cricket and they went to nick cars. My friends in Preston were those I met through the New Friargate social club with my brother."

But the lure of the pick 'n' mix counter was no match when England Under-19s came knocking in early 1995. They were touring the West Indies and he went originally as a batsman, a replacement for Owais Shah – another future senior international – who couldn't get a passport quickly enough. But by the end he was batting number nine and opening the bowling. "I ended up knackering my back up properly. I couldn't get the ball out of my hands to be honest. People kept getting injured and I just carried on and I think one week I bowled pushing 100 overs. I got home and my back just collapsed."

The coach on that tour was David Lloyd, who became an energetic cheerleader for Flintoff, probably for life. He had seen the future when he watched Flintoff make a duck against the wonderful West Indian quick bowler Malcolm Marshall opening the batting for St Anne's against Preston. Lloyd told Pat Murphy: "Marshall bowled him fifth ball, but it remains the best nought I've ever seen. He had time to play and looked composed against a great fast bowler."

And it was Lloyd, in his guise as Lancashire coach, who had gone to the Flintoff house "all polite" and talked his mum and dad around over tea and biscuits in the front room that summer. Flinoff waved goodbye to Preston with a two-year contract in his pocket. It soon became three. He had never watched Lancashire before he joined the club, now Old Trafford was to be his seond home.

Lloyd proceeded to laud Flintoff to the gnarled old pros in the Lancashire dressing room, which raised a few eyebrows. Sure enough, when the time came for his debut against Hampshire in late August 1995, he blew it. He didn't get out of single figures and dropped three catches standing at second slip to the booming swing bowling of Wasim Akram, who was leading the side and had steam coming out of his ears at the end of his run-up. Flintoff later said that: "Funnily enough, it was more nerve-wracking than playing for England."

Others remember him for different reasons. The Reverend Malcolm Lorimer, the Lancashire chaplain, recalls him as a new boy. "I just couldn't get over what he looked like. Most of the young lads are scrawny and fill out later, but he already had huge shoulders which was very unusual. I thought to myself, good grief, he *will* be able to hit the ball."

The Lancashire dressing room was an intimidating place to be, stuffed with men who had played for England or other countries, a place where you had to knock on the first-team door before being allowed in.

"It was daunting. I didn't say anything for about three years," says Flintoff. "You would go in and look around and there were people you had seen on telly. You didn't know what to say to them, you just sat there and waited to be spoken to."

But after a time, he learnt to raise his head, to share a beer or three and he got to know them, and found a good friend and a mentor in Neil Fairbrother, who was to have a huge impact on his career. He is now his manager and helps keep the chaotic Flintoff roadshow on the go.

County cricket was not easy, though. Flintoff played only five County Championship games between the beginning of 1995 and the end of 1997. It was not going to be a heady ride to glory. His back was suspect and his batting was not steady enough to gain him a place as a specialist. Lancashire were still striving for their first outright championship win since 1934 and competition was fierce. And then Dav Whatmore, an Australian who had made his name by coaching Sri Lanka's shock 1996 World Cup winners, took over from Lloyd in 1997 without the same soft spot for Flintoff, thinking him a scallywag or worse.

Flintoff's maiden championship century came at last at Southampton in July 1997. It was a biff-a-minute Flintoff special containing one six and 22 fours and he felt he had really achieved something at last. A watching Matthew Hayden, then a Hampshire player, said he had never seen an Australian teenager hit the ball as hard or as cleanly, but after a pair against Derbyshire in his next match, he was back in the seconds. Against

Chapter opener: From little acorns, giant oaks grow...
Left: Andrew Flintoff in 1992, aged 15.

Yorkshire Second XI he tried to smash Gareth Batty into the stratosphere and was out. Furious, he thumped the wall of the dressing room as hard as he could and broke his hand. Aged 19, he was out for the season and out of favour.

All this time he had been playing England age-group cricket with people like Alex Tudor, his Under-11 rival, who was to crop up at crucial intervals in his career. Flintoff's back hindered his bowling progress, but he was good enough for the then 17-year-old Michael Vaughan to wonder how far he himself could go because "there was this young cricketer who made things look easy."

After an England schools tour of South Africa, he bypassed the Under-17s completely and joined the England Under-19s to tour the West Indies, Zimbabwe and Pakistan over three consecutive winters. The side he led in Pakistan, and which won the Test series 1–0, were hailed by Mudassar Nazar, who was managing Pakistan Under-19s, as "the best touring side, including senior Test teams, ever to tour the country". Flintoff also impressed with his demeanour, maturity and inter-personal skills.

He had on his hands a quick bowler of devastating potential – Steve Harmison of Durham. He was very fast, very tall and with an action coaches fantasize over. However Harmison, on his first trip away from the north east, was suffering from crippling homesickness. Flintoff spent many hours comforting his team-mate and said that if he still felt the same in two days he could fly back home. Two days later he did, but from the long hours of talking, a firm friendship was forged which was to help both them and England as their careers developed. Robert Key also became a good mate.

Alex Tudor, who was also on that tour of Pakistan, told Pat Murphy: "I was very impressed with the mature way he spoke at the functions. No notes, he ad-libbed a lot and was very popular with our hosts. We were all very proud of our captain. In one game on that tour, I was being bombarded by rocks on the boundary and Freddie firmly told the umpires that he wasn't having that. He was all set to take us off and the umpires made the police go into the crowd and sort it out. The stadium was packed, but Freddie wouldn't compromise."

Kate Laven, a sportswriter, who has followed Flintoff's career closely, remembers her first dealings with him. "He was captain of the Under-19s when Zimbabwe toured here in 1997. He got a hundred before lunch in the first Test and it was just an awesome innings. I thought, bloody hell, this boy can play. You could just tell that he had the potential to be special. It was not just his batting, he had an instinct for the game that set him apart from everyone else. I remember talking to him afterwards, he was a bit shy, a bit cheeky and a bit uncertain in his dealings with the media."

That summer Flintoff's team-mate, friend and rival Ben Hollioake was plucked from the Under-19s to play against Australia in the Ashes. There were plenty of whispers that Flintoff wasn't far off. In fact he had rather outshone Hollioake in the second Under-19 one-day international by scoring 72.

The following winter he was on the England A tour of Sri Lanka and Kenya. When a bomb exploded in Kandy, Flintoff was one of the few who spoke out in favour of staying in Sri Lanka. Kate Laven was there and remembers the personality behind the cricketer. "Flintoff was doing a column for the local paper and he used to ask me to look at it for him. He was obviously quite a bright bloke, it was really nicely written, with good points and not just a travelogue. He is much more intelligent on paper than he appeared to be with the spoken word. He really is one of the nicest cricketers and is unusual in the way that he will ask about you; you can have a proper two-way conversation with him."

Back injuries limited his opportunities on the tour, but the wires were still buzzing. *The Daily Telegraph*'s assessment was: "Built like a rugby union No. 8 with power to match, but hits straight. Savage puller. Bullet-like throw. Big potential."

Simon Hughes, later the Channel 4 analyst but then in the early stages of his transition from player to journalist, wrote: "Just how much he'll make fielders fingers tingle and bowlers' necks rick when he is big enough to start shaving, just doesn't bear thinking about."

Left: By the age of 19, Flintoff was already established in the Lancashire team and winning honours, including this Player of the Month award for August 1997.

England's
SAVIOUR?

Spring 1998, and the groundstaff are planting the hanging baskets outside the Old Trafford pavilion. If they had leant on their forks, nodded sagely and told the passing Andrew Flintoff that he would play in two Tests by the end of the year, he would have playfully clubbed them with one of his giant paws. But these were difficult times for English cricket and, by mid-summer, the selectors were looking around for answers.

England had toured the West Indies unsuccessfully in the winter, and seemed to be hurtling towards defeat against South Africa after following on at Lord's and just avoiding defeat at Old Trafford. The country had gone football World Cup crazy, there were empty seats at the Tests and calls for new blood were increasing.

Meanwhile, Flintoff's summer had started promisingly in a freezing April when he top-scored in both the AXA League and County Championship games against Sussex. At last he had won a more permanent place in both the Lancashire championship and one-day sides – the coach Dav Whatmore had softened a little towards his young man mountain.

"He is less idle and better at utilizing his time, thinks about the game the night before and is paying more attention to his performance," Whatmore told *The Times*. "He is going to frustrate me and his team-mates, but he fits in very well in the dressing room and is capable of going the distance."

There was widespread support for Flintoff in the dressing room too, and before long the captain started cranking up the praise. Wasim Akram called for Flintoff to play for his country: "He is good enough to play for England right now. If he were Pakistani he would be in our side. England have always been reluctant to promote young talent... but I say get them in when they're teenagers and they have no fear."

Lancashire also started promoting their floodlit one-day games solely on the basis of Flintoff's power, which worried team-mate Michael Atherton.

At the beginning of June, Flintoff made a century against Northamptonshire, his huge forearms beating the ball to all corners of Wantage Road, and, on 21 June, he had his moment in the sun.

Lancashire were playing Surrey at Old Trafford and, on the Sunday evening, they were galloping towards a victory target of 253 at five an over. The young Surrey pace bowler Alex Tudor was bowling to Flintoff, who decided to chance his arm. The over went 6, 4, 4, 4, 4, 6, 6, 0 – 34 runs, which, with two no-balls, made it the second most expensive over in first-class history. As well as a niche in cricket folklore, those eight balls perhaps won Flintoff his first Test cap.

There were more pyrotechnics in the next match against Warwickshire at Edgbaston – a 70 including eight fours and two sixes in a run chase – and his back was holding up sufficiently for him to get through a few overs. The whispers were that here was the new saviour of English cricket. And the whispers reached important ears.

The call came on the way to a benefit game for Wasim Akram. Mike Watkinson, then one of Flintoff's senior colleagues and now the Lancashire coach, heard his phone ringing. It was David Graveney. He asked to speak to Flintoff, who didn't have a phone of his own and thought that Watkinson was winding him up. He wasn't – Flintoff was in the squad for the fourth Test at Trent Bridge, the Nottingham ground where a young Ian Botham had made his Test debut 21 years earlier. Flintoff had taken the place of Ben

Chapter opener: The fresh-faced debutant prepares for his first Test match v South Africa at Trent Bridge in July 1997; Right: Catching practice with captain Mike Atherton.

Hollioake, who had been dropped from the squad after some faltering mid-summer form.

He had played only 15 championship matches and taken eight first-class wickets. England had taken the punt that Wasim had urged.

The morning of the Test came and Flintoff was in the team. At 20, he was the youngest Lancashire player to represent England. By the time the Test came along, Flintoff had lost some of his early season pizzazz but the buzz got to him. He took one for 52 in the first innings, bowling at a brisk medium pace, despite his painful back. He batted at eight, and Michael Atherton later wrote that Flintoff was so relaxed he might have been playing for his club. "When I went out I felt really good and I got out being a bit overconfident," said Flintoff. "I tried to hit Jacques Kallis over extra-cover for six and was caught behind."

His reception on his return to the pavilion was chilly. This was not a dressing room full of camaraderie, rather players whose insular attitude was perhaps understandable given the selectors' readiness to chop and change and the carrot of an Ashes tour dangling in front of them. It was a very different atmosphere to Old Trafford and Flintoff reverted to his old, shy self.

England won the Test, thanks to a titanic innings by Michael Atherton featuring a classic duel with Allan Donald, and Flintoff kept his place for the next match at Headingley.

There, in front of a Yorkshire crowd, he had one of the worst moments of his career – when he followed his first-innings duck with another in the second. He trudged off forlorn. "I had a tear in my eye," he said, "and I went and hid in the sauna for three hours."

But another victory meant that Flintoff's first two Tests had been winning ones – which was pretty unusual at the time. He said afterwards: "Some people have asked if you feel part of the victory celebrations when you scored nought in both innings and failed to take a wicket. I can only speak for myself, but too right I did. I was drinking champagne with the rest of the lads."

But the experience, though exciting, hadn't been a particularly happy one. The coaches had fiddled around with his run-up and batting technique the day before his first Test and, to make things worse, someone pinched his England cap at Headingley. It was to be his last taste of international cricket for a while – he was dropped for the final Test of the summer against Sri Lanka and the Ashes squad came and went without a mention of his name. He later said that maybe he was picked too soon.

But England had not forgotten him and he was selected for the England A tour of Zimbabwe and South Africa in the new year. The captain was a young Yorkshire player called Michael Vaughan.

Back at Old Trafford, Lancashire were having a great season. They finished runners-up in the championship and, on 6 September, won the NatWest Trophy against Derbyshire. The next day they won the AXA League, thus clinching their third Double of the 1990s. Flintoff was awarded his county cap and voted the Cricket Writers' Club Young Player of the Year.

The A tour to Zimbabwe and South Africa that winter was a successful one for Flintoff the batsman – he topped the averages with 542 runs at 77.42 including one century and five fifties. He enjoyed playing under the captaincy of Vaughan, rating him as a wise and relaxed leader. Vaughan too learnt important lessons about Flintoff, about how to motivate and get the best out of the team talisman.

Flintoff's bowling, however, was another story. His back hurt, again, but the management decided that he should be given cortisone injections to keep him going. In his autobiography, *Being Freddie*, he said. "The treatment I was given was barbaric. I braced both hands against the wall and the 'specialist' just stuck the needle into my back without an anaesthetic. After six injections, I was able to bowl for the rest of that tour at least."

It earnt him selection for the World Cup squad – the competition was due to be held in Britain in May. He flew off to Sharjah, United Arab Emirates, for a warm-up tournament and made a run-a-ball 50 on his debut. He also fielded brilliantly and his World Cup place was guaranteed, despite a night on the booze the evening before the team returned

Previous pages: The first of many... South African Jacques Kallis becomes Flintoff's first-ever Test match victim at Trent Bridge, July 1997.

which left him climbing onto the airport bus in a blazer and tie but no shirt.

The World Cup was supposed to dominate that summer, it was supposed to make England fall in love with cricket again. In fact, that moment was to be a Test series six years in the distance.

Flintoff though was hitting prime form at the start of the season. On 25 April, he battered the Essex attack in the CGU competition – largely over long on and long off – for 143 off 66 balls. Pat Gibson in *Wisden Cricket Monthly* described how umpire Nigel Plews "became the first umpire to signal a no-ball with his head tucked under his arm" as Flintoff rocketed Ashley Cowan straight back for four.

As the aftershocks rocked Chelmsford, Mike Watkinson shook his head in wonder. "I bowled to Viv Richards," he said. "I bowled to Ian Botham and, as a youngster, I played with Clive Lloyd. This boy hits a cricket ball harder than any of them."

By the beginning of May, England's tub-thumping artery Darren Gough was asking people not to expect too much of Flintoff during the World Cup.

He shouldn't have worried. Flintoff batted in only two of England's five games, and did not make much of an impression with the ball, as they slipped out of the competition at the first stage thanks to an unfathomably poor run rate. By 30 May it was all over, with *The Sun* saying, "Let's get this in proportion – this was only the most catastrophic day ever for English cricket."

Flintoff's great supporter as England coach, David Lloyd, resigned, as did the captain Alec Stewart. On his return to Lancashire, Flintoff picked up a bat he had borrowed from Alec Stewart after his own had been stolen during England's final debacle against India at Edgbaston and scored a century before lunch against Gloucestershire at Bristol. It took him 61 balls.

Then, at Scarborough in August, he hit another century before lunch, becoming the first Lancashire player to score a hundred in a Roses match before the crab salads had been served. Not much happened in between, but as *Wisden* observed, 'he looked a star in the making."

Lancashire finished the season runners-up in the championship for the second year in a row and as winners of the inaugural National League competition. There had been persistent whispers that Flintoff wanted to leave Old Trafford for greener pastures, and more money. Flintoff always vociferously denied them and, in the autumn, he signed a new one-year contract with Lancashire, with a three-year option.

England's new captain-coach team of Nasser Hussain and Duncan Fletcher, were rebuilding after a disastrous series against New Zealand which followed the World Cup and which ranked them officially as the worst team in the world. They had chosen a young fresh team to start the process.

It was a long, hard tour. It started at Johannesburg with England 2 for 4 after three overs. Flintoff made 38 – the highest score of the innings – before being tempted into a rash shot by Lance Klusener. It was a familiar dismissal – he still hadn't learnt how to resist having a thrash when his adrenalin was pumping.

However, by the second Test, his batting had improved, he was learning not to swing across the line against high-class fast bowling. His bowling was also slipping nicely into place after initial worries that he would have to go home because of a bad back.

By the next Test, in Durban, Nasser Hussain was moved to salute Flintoff. "I'm excited by his fitness levels, he's now doing exactly what we wanted him to do," he said. "To get into the England side he's got to be an all-rounder who bowls 15 overs a day and gets wickets, and that is what he is doing.

"I'm excited about his professionalism and the way he can hit a cricket ball. For a long time we've lacked a number seven batsman who can come in and take the game by the scruff of the neck."

But not long into the New Year, when things were beginning to click into place, he broke a bone in his left foot in the fourth Test – he would be out for ten weeks. He flew home. He had talked on tour about how his cricket had "always been about peaks and troughs". Over the next two years he was to experience the deepest trough of his career.

the
WEIGHT
of expectation

Curry, chips and a few pints have fuelled many a downfall. But few can have been as public as Andrew Flintoff's in the summer of 2000.

The young Flintoff had been a beanpole, tall and with broad shoulders, but lean as a lath until he was 19. But then a natural filling-out and change in lifestyle kicked in. After a couple of years at Old Trafford, he decided to leave the bright lights of Preston and his parents and move into a loft apartment in Manchester with a couple of friends. He was good-looking, had spare money, friends, admiration from girls and a thirst. He was never an aggressive drunken yob, but felt the draw of the late-night kebab shop like many of his contemporaries. The Australian Stuart Law, no mean drinker himself, later described to an Australian newspaper the experience of being "Freddied".

Flintoff had not noticed that he had put on weight – whenever he looked in the mirror it was just the same old reflection, but others, in influential positions, had. He was prone to collecting a few extra pounds and struggling to keep them off. And that, combined with a feeling that he just wasn't performing to his potential and that his excess weight was hampering his bowling, was driving the frustration of some in the England camp to virtual boiling point.

Flintoff returned from the previous winter's tour of South Africa early, with a remodelled batting stance, but had done well enough to remain in Duncan Fletcher's thoughts. He was picked for the first two Tests against Zimbabwe in the summer of 2000 and then the first-innings defeat by the West Indies at Edgbaston. But he failed to thrive and, after a bad back (again) put him out of the sensational Lord's Test before it started, he was sent back to Old Trafford.

It was then, in mid-summer, that the whispers about his weight started, and they multiplied during the triangular one-day series with the West Indies and Zimbabwe. He missed a game early in the tournament because of his back and the ball started rolling. He woke up one morning in July to find that his weight had made it onto the back pages under headlines like "Vast bowler" and "Fat boy". *The Sun* famously mocked up a picture of Flintoff next to Lennox Lewis, the ex-world heavyweight boxing champion, claiming that Flintoff, with his weight now topping 19 stone, was two pounds heavier.

There had been a leak from somewhere in Team England – the bubble which supposedly protected the players from the press – to the piranhas of the back pages. There were no straight denials and even the inscrutable Duncan Fletcher said when questioned: "He's under a lot of pressure and he knows he has a point to prove."

Flintoff was mortified. He later admitted: "I wasn't small, but no-one had been telling me to lose weight. It was just so embarrassing.

"It seemed to come out of the blue, it was also unsettling. I don't mind criticism if I get out to a daft shot, but personal criticism is uncalled for... it wasn't as if I was a blimp. They made out I was letting the whole country down because I had a few extra pounds."

For two weeks he hid – he thought that people were looking in his trolley when he was shopping at the supermarket and staring and pointing when he walked down the street. He was unable to train because of his back. His parents were upset, his friends didn't know where to look and, for a short time, he wondered if being a professional cricketer

Chapter opener: Flintoff's weight issues made headlines in summer 2000; Right: An "awesome" innings of 135 not out for Lancashire v Surrey drew plaudits from David Gower, though.

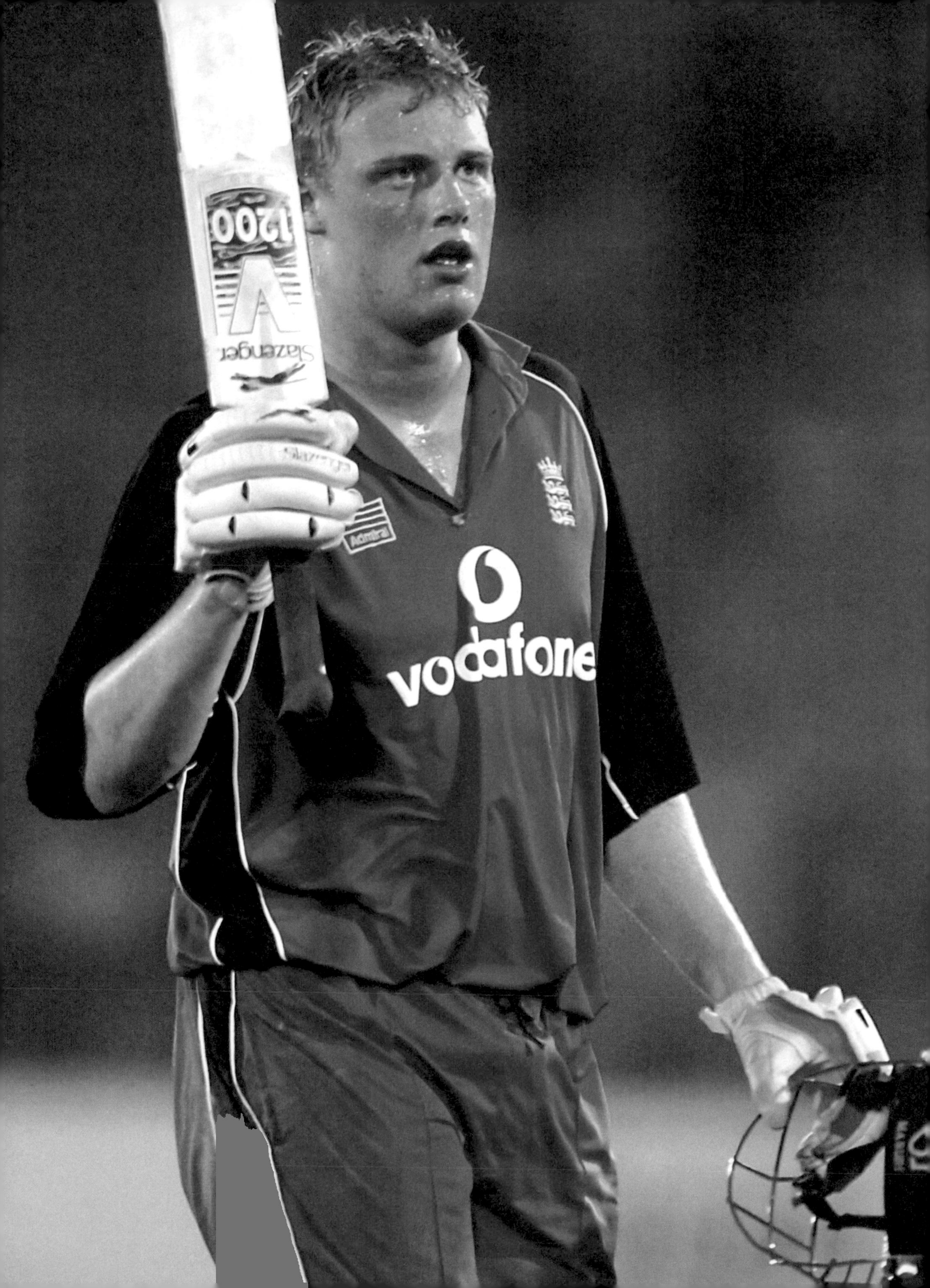

1200
V
Slazenger
Admiral
vodafone

was worth the hassle. When he went out for a drink with a mate, a tabloid reported that he had been as drunk as a skunk. By the time he played for England against Zimbabwe at Old Trafford on 13 July, his confidence was shattered.

He went out to bat without his back support, even though he needed it, because he thought it would make him look bigger. It was England's first home game under lights, but Flintoff ensured that they didn't need to use much electricity by whacking 42 off 45 balls to win England the game. He didn't enjoy it though. "It was a horrible feeling," he said. "I felt everybody was looking at me. People were shouting things from the crowd." He twice walloped spinner Paul Strang over the ropes and those in charge of the Lancashire PA system might not have helped Flintoff's mood by playing "Sex Bomb" to celebrate, however well-intentioned. England won by eight wickets and during the post-match interview, after he had won the Man of the Match award, he muttered to the television reporter: "Not bad for a fat lad."

Then, just a couple of weeks later, Flintoff made his critics cringe again. It was the NatWest quarter-final at The Oval, Lancashire against the eventual County Championship winners, Surrey. Flintoff found himself walking in with the score 0 for 1. He hit the first ball for four – clipped to the square-leg boundary – and from then onwards made the Surrey attack, including Saqlain Mushtaq and Alex Tudor, look as if they'd just been pulled off Blackpool beach. He finished 135 not out off 111 balls and David Gower, a pundit not known for hyperbole, told Sky's viewers: "We have just watched one of the most awesome innings we are ever going to see on a cricket field."

Flintoff was chuffed, especially as the game had been seen by thousands on television, who could make their own minds up about his ability, chubby or not. He said afterwards: "It was just one of those days when it all worked, everything happened as you would want it to."

After that the season petered to an end – Lancashire were second in the championship again, but their run of one-day success had come to an end. Flintoff's season had had its highs, but also its lows. Neil Fairbrother says in *Flintoff: My Life in Pictures*: "He found regular failure very hard to take. He seemed to be making the same mistakes with the bat time and time again. It was slow progress in those years. At Durham, in the summer of 2000, he twice got himself out cheaply. He lay in the bath and I thought that he was going to drown himself."

That autumn, Flintoff tried again to get himself into shape. He had an operation to numb the nerves in his back and spent a lot of time in the gym with advice from the former Wigan and Great Britain rugby league full-back Steve Hampson, who was then coaching the Preston-based Lancashire Lynx club. He tried to modify his bowling action to put less stress on his back. He also went out running with his two much-loved pet boxers – Freddie and a rescue dog called Arnold. He started taking diet tablets, cut out beer and, perhaps most importantly, he tried to stop the injections.

In September 2000 he said: "I've had ten cortisone injections now, and everyone says I should not have too many of those. I was apprehensive about the last one, but I went along and had it done. I've decided not to have any more, and I'm going to remain firm on that because I'm only 22 and have to think about the future."

He went with England to Kenya for the ICC Trophy and then on to Pakistan and Sri Lanka. As usual, nothing was straightforward. In the first one-day international at Karachi he made 84 off 60 balls to heave England to victory with their first 300-plus total. He was the Man of the Match. Yet not five days earlier he had been told that he would have to fly home before the Test matches because he had not proved his fitness as a bowler. His back was playing up again.

England called up his old mate Alex Tudor as a replacement and Duncan Fletcher started talking in terms which suggested that he was losing faith in Flintoff's long-term ability to bowl. "Depending on what comes back from further investigations on his back problem, the decision has then got to be made by him," Fletcher said. "He may have an operation

Left: Despite a bad back, Flintoff powered a match-winning 84 off 60 balls in England's first one-day international against Pakistan in winter 2000.

or he may decide against it and just leave it and try and bowl again in three years, but he will have lost out on a lot of experience by then... I think he could have been a very effective all-rounder."

It was not a happy time.

Flintoff flew home after the one-day series, but he had not had time to unpack his suitcase before he was summoned back as a specialist batsman following injuries to Michael Vaughan and Nasser Hussain. When he arrived at the Lahore hotel, there was only one room left... and two people who needed it – Flintoff and David Graveney, the chairman of selectors. Flintoff took the floor. The very next day his nose was smashed by a local net bowler in his first practice session and he didn't play a Test.

Later in the New Year he flew out to Sri Lanka to shore up the one-day team. He arrived with a strained left ankle, an injury sustained in a kickabout during pre-season training with Lancashire. England complained they had been left uninformed, while Lancashire countered that the complaint from England was the first they knew about it. The series came and went with Flintoff making minimal impact.

The 2001 season was a miserable one. The Australians emphatically retained the Ashes, but Flintoff was nowhere near selection. He later admitted: "I shouldn't even have been playing for Lancashire." Lancashire's season itself drifted into mediocrity – they only avoided relegation by flying Muttiah Muralitharan in for the last match of the year. The dressing room was split between the Old Trafford establishment and the captain John Crawley and coach Bobby Simpson, formerly in charge of the Australian team. Flintoff, though at last managing to bowl more quickly and more reliably, was struggling for runs. Lancashire continued to show great trust in him, but he made only two fifties in the entire championship season. And during the summer Simpson had called him into his office, sworn at him and then walked out.

Another season had drifted by and the end was celebrated with a six-wicket loss in the Norwich Union League to bottom-of-the-table Derbyshire.

The next day Flintoff was told by his management team – his Lancashire team-mate Neil Fairbrother and Andrew "Chubby" Chandler of the International Sports Management group – to come to Old Trafford for a meeting. Flintoff's ears were blown off. This was bad cop, worse cop.

According to *The Sunday Times*, Fairbrother said: "Face the lockers. I want you to look at John's [Crawley] spot first. This is how a professional cricketer keeps his kit. Okay, Freddie now let's take a look at yours. It's a pile of shit. You seem to have the impression that you can just saunter in and turn it on. You can't Freddie. You've got to be better prepared."

They made their frustration at his lifestyle and attitude clear. They questioned his professionalism and whether he still had the burning desire to do what it took to get back into the England side. They told him to stop working himself up about his weight and face the fact that some of the criticism was justified.

Flintoff sat and listened. He would not have taken it from many people, but he admired his interrogators and knew in his heart that they were right. "I was drifting along, not going anywhere, probably believing I was doing the right thing but wasn't, probably kidding myself. So they sat me down and gave me a few home truths about how I was going to improve my game."

The three of them started to formulate a plan about how he was going to resurrect his England Test career. He had been picked for the one-day teams due to tour Zimbabwe at the beginning of the autumn and India after Christmas, but he needed some focus in between.

At Fairbrother's suggestion, the next day he rang Duncan Fletcher and asked if he could go, at his own expense, to the England Academy in Adelaide – for 6am starts, cold showers and iron discipline from the ex-Australian wicket-keeper and whip-cracker extraordinaire, Rod Marsh. Fletcher, in his own quiet way, agreed and Flintoff, unknowingly, had taken the first and biggest step on the road to self-worth and superstardom on the cricket field and beyond.

Left: After being called back to Pakistan as a specialist batsman in November 2000, Flintoff's nose was smashed by a local net bowler during his first practice session.

fitter, happier, more
PRODUCTIVE

And it was in India, beautiful, crazy India, a doom-laden place for many a heavy-footed fast bowler, that the renaissance started. Flintoff couldn't bat, couldn't get a run, but he bowled fast and with great heart. And throughout that winter of 2001–02, the progress continued. It was the beginning of a new beginning, a period of slow but steady progress that left him believing that perhaps he could be an international cricketer. He won an extended run in the Test team for the first time and the transformation was there for anyone to see.

But being in India for the Test series in November was not part of the Fairbrother-Chandler plan. At that showdown meeting at Old Trafford, they had set Flintoff the target of the Zimbabwe one-day tour and a scrub-the-floor stint at the new Academy.

England arrived in Zimbabwe in early October with a young squad. The tour had been organized by Duncan Fletcher to try and boost the morale of a one-day side which was faltering after losing all six games to Pakistan and Australia that summer. They were also trying to plan for the World Cup which was to be held in Southern Africa early in 2003.

Fletcher's native country were pretty hopeless – beset by money disputes, racial disputes, contract disputes and a country that was slowly disintegrating about their ears. But Zimbabwe were a bit of a bogey team for England, so although England's 5–0 win came as no surprise, it was an intense relief.

When Flintoff won the first match in Harare with a six, it was England's first one-day win for 344 days and 11 matches. The series grew increasingly acrimonious, and perhaps meaningless, but Flintoff was enjoying himself. He later called the two weeks he spent there a "lifeline". He never bowled his full allocation of overs in a game, but he was quick and aggressive. His batting was big-hitting yet restrained and, by the last match of the series in Bulawayo, even the schoolchildren bussed in by the Zimbawe Cricket Union were shouting his name.

Duncan Fletcher hailed him as the find of the tour. David Lloyd, who had been watching carefully from the sidelines, also saw real progress in his progeny. "He has to work on his bowling variation and his shot selection, but it looks as if the penny has finally dropped," Lloyd said. "He has shown a glimpse of the fantastic potential."

From Zimbabwe, Flintoff was off to the Academy. This imitation of the successful Australian version was conceived by the ECB as the feeding ground for an England side that they planned to be the best in the world by 2007.

It was originally to be built at Bisham Abbey before planning problems forced a switch to Loughborough – but for the moment it was just a pile of rubble. So this first intake were going to the hot sun of Adelaide for 16 weeks. However, anyone who thought that they were in for a pleasant few weeks of larking around in the heat were in for a shock. Before the students arrived, Rod Marsh, who had overseen the Australian Academy before accepting an offer to revive the Pommie enemy, told the press: "They're here to toughen up." That included physical jerks, lectures, yoga and doing their own washing.

Flintoff roomed with Steve Harmison and was ready for whatever was thrown at him, but it wasn't entirely what he had hoped for. He later told Michael Atherton: "It was different to what I expected. I only batted about four times and didn't really progress technically."

A continent away though, things were gathering

Chapter opener: Hard work and a more responsible attitude got Flintoff back on track.
Right: Punting with Matthew Hoggard in Christchurch, New Zealand, March 2002.

44

apace. England's autumn tour of India had been an on-off affair, with security concerns in light of the 9/11 attacks on America preying on the minds of the players. Darren Gough and Alec Stewart had already chosen to take the tour off to spend time with their families, then Andy Caddick and Robert Croft pulled out because of worries about terrorism. This makeshift squad became more confused when Craig White, England's senior all-rounder, admitted to the England camp after being in India for about a week, that he was no longer a strike bowler – that he couldn't touch speeds of 90 mph any more. England had a young, inexperienced and not very quick bowling attack on their hands.

Fletcher consulted with Hussain and decided that they needed an addition to the strike force – a strong man to bang the ball into the pitch and supplement the squad – and the name that came up, inconceivable a few months ago, was Flintoff.

"We picked the Test squad before Zimbabwe and the big thing we noticed out there was his attitude," said Fletcher. "There was a lot more responsibility about him, he has lost weight and the reports from the Academy have also been good. Now it looks as if we really need him here. He bowled very quickly in Zimbabwe and at the back end of the season for his county."

Flintoff woke up in Adelaide one morning at 6.30am, went online and there was an email demanding his presence in India. He assured Fletcher that his back was "105 percent" better and arrived in time to stride into the apricot dust and painted splendour of the Jaipur cricket ground where England were due to play India A. The Indians immediately warmed to this blond giant with a shimmering earring.

After a nets session, in the luxury of the team hotel, an old palace where peacocks fluttered on the lawn, Flintoff spoke to the press. He sat on a cane chair on the cool veranda and contemplated what had happened.

"I'm working a lot harder with my game than I ever was," he said. "I realized that I was just drifting for a while and now I'm just desperately trying to get back into the Test team.

"Last year I probably worked as hard at my game as I ever had and probably had the worst season I've ever had, which was a bit disillusioning for a while, but I worked hard in Zimbabwe and it seemed to pay off. I thought I played all right without breaking any real pots."

When asked if he'd be prepared to open the bowling, he said: "I'd do anything to be honest. If I had to open the bowling, that would be great. I took the new ball once for England, for two overs in a Test match against the West Indies at Edgbaston."

It was more experience than any of the rest of the team had.

He did well in his first game, the penultimate before the start of the series, taking six wickets and making a rapid 40 in the second innings as England notched up what was to be their only first-class win of the tour. He had done enough and was in the team for the first Test at Mohali – which was itself in question almost until the moment Sourav Ganguly and Nasser Hussain turned up for the toss because of a dispute between the Indian board of control and the International Cricket Council.

England lost heavily, mainly because they seemed cast in iron boots when faced with the Indian spin twins, Anil Kumble and Harbhajan Singh, who took 15 easy wickets between them. But Flintoff, who celebrated his 24th birthday during the game, bowled his heart out. Angus Fraser, the ex-England bowler and toiler, now writing for *The Independent,* was impressed enough to write a note saying it was the best nought-for he'd ever seen in a Test, and slip it under the door of Flintoff's hotel room. Flintoff's reward was to share the new ball with another greenhorn, Yorkshire's Matthew Hoggard, in the next two Tests.

He enjoyed the experience, bowling fast and hard, even if the tactics he implemented didn't impress many commentators. Nasser Hussain, faced with the intractable problem of Sachin Tendulkar, decided to implement his own brand of leg theory. That meant Flintoff banging the ball in short from around the wicket and Ashley Giles bowling his left-arm spin over the wicket and firing

Previous pages: Flintoff scores another run on his way to his maiden Test hundred and a partnership of 291 with Graham Thorpe against Christchurch, New Zealand, March 2002.

wide of leg-stump. It wasn't pretty and though it slowed Tendulkar, there was no great victory – he still finished with an average of 76 and with significantly more runs than anyone on either side.

Flintoff's batting on the other hand disintegrated to the extent that watching him walking out to the middle became an addictive horror peep-show. He would stomp out, his body language terrible, swish at a spinner and walk back to jeers. He made just 26 runs in five innings.

It completely knocked his confidence. Here was a cricketer who considered himself a batsman who bowled rather than the other way round and he couldn't get a run. He told *Wisden Cricket Monthly* afterwards: "I'm not a nervy cricketer, but there were times when I was waiting to go out to bat, that I really felt the pressure mounting."

When he bashed his fourth ball, from Sarandeep Singh, to midwicket for a duck in the final Test at Bangalore he went back to the dressing room for a good cry. "I was upset, just about off the planet, distraught. I'd started turning it around. I'd lost weight, I was bowling, I was working hard, but I couldn't score runs for love nor money. Letting the team down like that was awful. But sitting there then I realized that I still had a job to do, I had got a new ball and maybe I could redeem myself."

He did, taking four wickets in the gloom and winning the Man of the Match award. Sanjay Manjrekar, anchor of the Indian batting line-up in the 1980s and early 1990s, called his bowling a revelation.

It was Graham Dilley, the England bowling coach, who had comforted Flintoff at Bangalore. He worked on his action – trying to stop him leaning back during his delivery stride and to start using his front arm as a pendulum to create momentum. He was also kind, with constant words of encouragement and confidence.

England had lost the Test series 1–0, but after Christmas they were back and ready to play six one-day internationals.

India had been expecting to thrash their rather hapless limited-overs opponents but, after England came back at Delhi – a game during which Flintoff

made 52 and claims he was shot at by the crowd – it all came down to the final match in Mohali. Flintoff nurtured England through the end of their innings with a careful 40 (Hussain said that he had his "sensible head on") and was then handed the ball for the last over of the game when the pressure was on and India needed six with two wickets left. First Flintoff ran out Anil Kumble with a nifty kick onto the stumps and then, with two balls left, he bowled Javagal Srinath. So excited was he that he whipped off his blue No. 11 shirt, twirled it around his head like a new lasso and charged madly around the field, his very English torso on show, pursued by his jubilant team-mates.

A very happy Hussain told *wisden.com* afterwards: "I hope big Fred is not going to start a trend with his celebration at the end – fortunately for us he's lost a bit of timber in recent weeks, otherwise it could have been a frightening sight! Obviously with all that hard work in the gym he reckoned it was time to show the world his new-found pecs!

"But I can fully understand it – the boys were on a high. Only an hour earlier we had been losing – series and all – in front of 50,000 noisy fans. It was a great moment for the lads at the end – everyone loves Fred and we all tore after him when he took that final wicket. The morale has been fantastic throughout this tour, and this victory makes everything worthwhile."

Flintoff, who had only come to India back in November as a substitute – so ill-prepared that he had only one pair of pants with him – had become an integral part of both the Test and one-day teams. "They became my lucky pants," he said. "I ripped them up after India."

He left for New Zealand describing India as "awesome". Fletcher, not known for being gushy, almost sounded soft when he talked about Flintoff. "He has come good on this tour and it just shows that if you have a little bit of patience it sometimes pays off," he said. "He's now a really good example for other people who live in the comfort zone."

The New Zealand tour kicked off with the one-day internationals. Flintoff only really got into his stride in the fourth, at Auckland, where he

produced career-best figures of four for 17 and was Man of the Match.

It was the Test series where he came alive. He walked to the wicket in the second innings at Lancaster Park, Christchurch on a pair – with his batting again under the spotlight. In his first 13 balls he hit five fours and a six.

Graham Thorpe, Flintoff's partner, was mature and level-headed. He counselled Flintoff between deliveries, calming him down and building him up. After a risky thwack, Flintoff revealed in *My Life In Pictures* that Thorpe had come up to him and shouted in his ear: "Come on. You've had all this time without a hundred! There'll be plenty of days when you can't lay a bat on it!"

When the moment eventually came, just before tea with a top-edged hook off Craig McMillan over the wicket-keeper's head, Flintoff was dazed. At the non-striker's end he looked up at the scoreboard with his name on it, then looked again and thought: "Nah, that can't be right." When he got back into the dressing room for tea he was so excited he danced a jig.

But the scoreboard wasn't lying. The conditions, some said, were agreeable – the pitch was hard, the square boundaries were short and the New Zealand attack was without Chris Cairns who had injured his right kneecap. But a maiden Test century is a maiden Test century. When he came to the crease England led by only 187; by the time he fell it was 551. In a partnership of 291 he and Thorpe had secured the match... or so they thought.

What the game will be remembered for in 100 years time is Nathan Astle's amazing rearguard assault which nearly brought off a ridiculous win for New Zealand on the last afternoon. He knocked up cricket's fastest double hundred – going from 101 to 200 in 39 balls – and reduced England's lead to less than 100, and their mood to nervous terror, when he was caught behind slogging at Hoggard. England had won and the celebrations in Christchurch went on long into the night.

From there the squad moved on to Wellington. They were excited about what they might achieve but at half past ten on the third morning, came some terrible news. Ben Hollioake, touring as part of the one-day squad just a month ago, was dead. He had been killed in a car crash in Western Australia, driving home from a family dinner at the age of 24. England were devastated. Hollioake was not just a naturally talented cricketer but a lovely, popular man. Flintoff, who had grown up playing cricket with him, was shaken to the core.

"We were the same age, we played England junior cricket together, we always thought we'd be playing in the same side. It was just tragic the way it happened. I was the next to bat and nothing else really mattered."

Both teams stood for a minute's silence the next day and the game went on in a bit of a daze. Flintoff made a 33-ball fifty in the second innings but no-one's heart was really in it and the game petered out into a draw. The tour came to a disappointing end at Auckland when England lost by 78 runs under the glare of floodlights – their first Test loss in New Zealand for 18 years.

But for Flintoff, the long winter had been a major breakthrough. He was a better and more confident cricketer than he believed possible eight months earlier. He was thinner, fitter and in the gym every other day. He had a Test century under his belt; he'd done a semi-striptease in front of 50,000 Indians; and won Man of the Match awards. A reporter who interviewed him in Wellington found him reading Sebastian Faulks' acclaimed novel *Birdsong* – before the Academy, he hadn't read a book since leaving school.

"I've never been too good at debuts or making my mark immediately," he told *The Guardian*, after coming home from New Zealand. "It took me a while to do well for Lancashire, it's been a lot longer and harder for England. I feel I know now what is required to play for England, both in terms of commitment and levels of skill."

But he was not the sort of man to get too cocky: "I don't think you'll ever crack this game," he went on. "I'm trying not to get carried away with what happened. I still feel I'm playing for my place. That 130 was great. But all I've got is a starting point, I've got a lot of building to do from there."

Left: Slimline Freddie shows off his new-found pecs to celebrate England's thrilling win in the sixth one-day international against India which tied the 2002 series 3–3.

LOVE
changes everything

The best thing to happen to Andrew Flintoff in the summer of 2002 was love. He met Rachael Wools, a marketing executive and former model, when playing for England against Sri Lanka at Edgbaston in early June. He liked her immediately and made it his mission to win her over.

He bought her a drink, informed her not entirely honestly that he had passed all his exams with an A, and told a few jokes. Then on the Sunday morning of the Test, Flintoff awoke to find a kiss-and-tell from a former fiancée, labelling him the England "all-bounder", staring at him from the pages of the *News of the World*. He hoped Rachael hadn't seen it. She had, but it didn't matter. They continued their courtship throughout the summer and were both hooked.

She said that she fell for him because "he made me laugh". He thought she was gorgeous, funny and clever.

Through a year speckled with disappointment and injury, she was a stable foundation, helping to keep him on the straight and narrow. She gave him something to strive for and when they later married and had a baby girl, something to come home to. He admitted in his autobiography that he found it difficult being alone, and would sometimes stay out late boozing just so that he didn't have to come back to an empty house. Now he rushes back to be with his family.

She has also been supportive of his career. "She's driven and that's helped me," he has said. "I'm driven too... She tries to organize me, we have come to a happy medium where I have improved and dragged her down a little bit to be a bit more laid back."

She helps him tune off from cricket. She has a career of her own and isn't really that interested in the minutiae of the game – it is a banned subject in the house. Flintoff even forbids any reminder of it on the walls, and refuses to read the papers, though Rachael flouted the ban to collect cuttings for a scrapbook for their daughter Holly.

Flintoff's agent Chubby Chandler, speaking to *The Guardian*, praised her to the hilt. "If anyone asked me what's changed his career, it's certainly her. I think he's genuinely happy and not just because he's scoring a lot of runs. His life is beginning to take really good shape."

But while his heart might have been beating wildly, Flintoff's body was about to fail him once again. In May, he played a championship match (his only one of the year) against Surrey, made a century and felt great. Then, on 7 June, Lancashire played and lost, by one wicket, to Warwickshire in the Benson and Hedges semi-final at Old Trafford. Flintoff was chuffed at having been appointed vice-captain of Lancashire, but began to feel a twinge in his groin as he bowled. He told England, who did nothing. So he played on.

He strode into the third Test against Sri Lanka, where he just kept bowling, thudding the ball into the pads of the batsman, and then into the triangular one-day series. Flintoff was one of the heartbeats of the side – taking nine wickets and making 190 runs at a strike rate of 129 including a formidable 40 in the final at Lord's where India won a thrilling victory. By then a twinge had become discomfort and by the end of the first Test against India, which England won and in which Flintoff made a fifty and was again worked heavily with the ball, pain had become agony. By the second Test against India at Trent Bridge, things had disintegrated to such a stage that he could barely walk and Rachael had to do up his

Chapter opener: Future wife Rachael brought balance to Freddie's life.
Right: An injury-ravaged Flintoff in thoughtful mode during a 2002–03 Ashes net session.

shoes. But still he had another injection and played, bowling 49 overs.

He felt so bad that he spoke to the management before the Headingley Test. But England were 1–0 up with two Tests to play and desperate to avenge their loss in India in 2001, so they told him to carry on. Those surrounding Flintoff were furious – he himself said in his autobiography that there was "unreasonable pressure put on me to play."

He played, of sorts, making a pair and somehow bowling 27 overs as England lost by an innings. It was not much of a surprise that he had failed to make an impact – he had difficulty getting out of his car. Eventually, England relented – he could miss the last Test at The Oval in early September and have his operation – a double hernia with staples put in either side of his groin.

The positive for Flintoff was that England had showed how much they now valued him, less than a year after he had been out in the cold. The negative side was that his career and long-term future had been put on the line. In order to get through the Indian series, they had risked the fact that he would not be fit to fly to Australia. Even the England captain Nasser Hussain later admitted that the treatment of Flintoff was "almost unprofessional" and that "it wouldn't have happened in most other sports."

Flintoff was named in the Ashes squad while recuperating under Dave "Rooster" Roberts, the Lancashire physiotherapist, with whom he negotiated the hills, fields and woods around Bolton. But England weren't satisfied, they wanted him where they could see him and he was told to report to the National Sports Centre at Lilleshall where he would be under direct England control. This is a place of which Michael Atherton wrote: "Quite frankly, three months in Wormwood Scrubs would be preferable. The stark, sparsely-furnished rooms are matched only by the dullness of the surrounding area."

But he worked there with Darren Gough – who was fighting to get fit after knee operations – and lots of footballers, from whom he heard countless tales of the perils of trying to play again too soon.

But by the time he flew out to Perth on 18 October, Flintoff still couldn't run. Duncan Fletcher was shocked by Flintoff's state when he arrived. England had been monitoring him back home so something had gone wrong somewhere in communications. In fact, England's tour party was rift by injuries – Gough's knee, Vaughan's knee, Trescothick's arm, Jones' rib. As *Wisden* commented: "The chief question was whether injured players had been given proper rehabilitation after surgery: the only possible answer had to be no."

Flintoff's first Ashes series was to turn into a nightmare. He was sent away to the National Academy in Adelaide to sort his injury out and though he trained hard, things just didn't seem to be getting any better. He had three MRI scans and an agonizing steroid injection "just above my old fella", played a couple of games – possibly too early – and was still not right. He didn't feel like he was getting a great deal of sympathy from the tour management despite the fact that if he had had his hernia operation earlier, he might now have been raring to go.

Warren Hegg, his new Lancashire captain, watching events from the north-west, was worried. "He should not even think about playing again until he and the medics are cast iron certain that his body can take the strain," he told the *Manchester Evening News*. "There are still exciting times in front of him and he mustn't risk them by pushing himself back into action too soon. That's a big danger for him. He is the sort of bloke who starts climbing up walls when he's not playing."

Three Tests came and went – England lost the series in 11 days – and Flintoff spent his 25th birthday wondering what had happened to his long-cherished dream. He hadn't played a Test, eventually he was ruled out of the one-day series and, at long last, two months after arriving, he was sent home to get fit for the World Cup. A gutted Flintoff flew out just as his parents set out to meet him and his brother on a long-planned family holiday. But at least he wasn't having to sit and

Previous pages: Flintoff talks to England coach Duncan Fletcher during the Australia tour of 2002–03. After two months, having not played a Test, he was sent home to get fit for the World Cup.

watch any more. In many ways it was a relief.

But he was flying back home into the lion's den. Lord MacLaurin, the outgoing chairman of the ECB, had told newspapers at the start of December that Flintoff "was doing things in his recuperation that he probably shouldn't have but that is between me, him and David Graveney (chairman of selectors). Professional footballers are back playing within four or five weeks".

Gough, for one, was furious, disgusted by MacLaurin's comments. "Andrew Flintoff is looking the best he has ever looked in his career and he trains hard every day," he said. "I was with him at the National Sports Centre at Lilleshall for a few weeks before the tour and he was working very hard. He had the surgery pretty late because, yet again, he was doing things to please England… A footballer is managed properly. They've a proper set-up."

And just as Flintoff was crossing the time zones, MacLaurin was at it again. "I had plenty of evidence to say that maybe Flintoff didn't do as much as he should have done. Well, he didn't, we knew that. It doesn't do any good when Darren Gough comes in and doesn't know what he is talking about."

But there had been no official complaint and none was put to the ECB's disciplinary committee. Even Tim Lamb, the chief executive of the ECB, sounded like he was trying to push clear blue water between him and the chairman. "Freddie himself has said that he worked as hard as he possibly could do at his rehab, and that has been borne out by the comments made by the physio and others who have had responsibility for looking after him," said Lamb. "You'll have to ask the chairman what evidence he's got… The quicker we draw a line in the sand under this whole bloody episode and move on from here the better, as far as I'm concerned." Duncan Fletcher seemed to back Flintoff as well, but the allegations didn't help his public image – Flintoff the beery layabout was back in people's perceptions, lying in the gutter and pissing away his dreams of playing for England.

When Flintoff arrived home he went straight back under the beady eye of Dave Roberts – where he had been three months earlier. He rented a flat in Altrincham and resolved to get well again. "I must admit there have been times when I've been quite down, but I must look forward to the World Cup. I have to forget about the Ashes," he told *The Times*. Again he and Roberts repaired to the Bolton countryside and the gym and occasional sessions with Oldham Football Club. Flintoff had never run as much in his life. It had to be relentless if he were to be fit for the World Cup – it began on 9 February in Cape Town, and countries had to name their squads by 31 December.

He was in the gym every day, apart from Christmas Day when it was closed. Then, he took his dogs for a long walk. Roberts also worked on building his shattered confidence and was fierce in Flintoff's defence. "Whoever said that [Flintoff had not rehabilitated properly] did not know or understand what he had actually done and the effects of that surgery," he told *The Times* in January. "You can print this: what they know about it I could write on a postage stamp. He's a six-foot-five, 17-and-a-half stone individual. People were saying others get back after four weeks. Well they might do if they're built like David Beckham but not when you're his size. There was a significant amount of muscle wastage around the injury that slowed down the process."

A meeting in Birmingham between England, the new chief medical officer Peter Gregory, Lancashire officials and Flintoff helped calm things down, though Chubby Chandler was still furious: "It's been a farce," he said.

In January 2003, Flintoff was checked over by the new medical officer and given the all-clear for the World Cup and, in the end, made the second final of the one-day series in Australia, flying back there on 17 January. England lost but he bowled through ten overs without pain. He has since stuck to the circuit-training programme Roberts gave him that miserable December and it has served him well.

The World Cup, a disaster for the home country South Africa, was to prove another disappointment for England. Their preparations were hampered by

CHAPTER SIX LOVE CHANGES EVERYTHING

indecision over whether or not to play their match against Zimbabwe. The players had been issued with death threats if they went, and others were concerned about the human rights abuses of the Mugabe government. The British government refused to make a political decision to stop the game going ahead and ECB officials failed to give much guidance. Nasser Hussain held endless meetings and, for a while, the team holed up in a hotel in Cape Town, surrounded by journalists waiting for a decision.

Eventually they decided not to go and forfeited four points. In theory they still had the firepower to make it through to the Super Six stage of the tournament. They thrashed Pakistan at Newlands, but were nearly embarrassed by JB Burger of Namibia, lost to India in Durban – though Flintoff did well with 64 and 2 for 15 – and were knocked out by Australia at Port Elizabeth.

It had been England's last game of the first round – they had to win to progress. And three-quarters of the way through that hot afternoon it seemed that they had done enough. After an early batting collapse in the face of Andy Bichel's rampant enthusiasm, Alec Stewart and Flintoff had helped England to a competitive total. Andy Caddick removed the Australian openers, others chipped in and the holders were 135 for 8 with 70 needed. But somehow, slowly, remorselessly, Bichel and Michael Bevan – the renowned one-day finisher – inched towards their target.

Poor James Anderson, Flintoff's young Lancashire team-mate, leaked runs in the penultimate over. Flintoff was given the last six balls to defend two runs and, after two dots, Michael Vaughan misfielded at mid-on. Alec Stewart could barely face his team-mates, Nasser Hussain was on his knees. Bichel – with seven for 20 and 34 not out – had the best day of his career. The Australian hoodoo continued and England's winter tour had ended in double failure.

The team mood was peculiar – united by the constant round of meetings about Zimbabwe and yet Flintoff described it as "tricky". Nasser Hussain resigned as one-day captain, to Duncan

Fletcher's dismay, at an emotional press conference in Port Elizabeth after hearing that rain had thwarted Pakistan's hopes of beating Zimbabwe – England's last chance of remaining in the competition. Australia went on to win the World Cup, thrashing India in the final.

But for Flintoff, the World Cup had been a quiet success, especially considering the traumas that had preceded it. His body had held up to the challenge of intense, short, sharp competition. He had mixed with the united nations of cricket and his boyhood hero Viv Richards had chatted to him about his batting for 20 minutes ("I couldn't believe he knew my name," he gushed).

He was also the most economical bowler in the tournament. By a mile. He took seven wickets at an economy rate of 2.88, including four for 78 in 28.4 overs against the stiff opposition of Pakistan, India and Australia. At his final press conference of the World Cup, Fletcher said: "Vaughan is a world-class Test player, [James] Anderson is coming through and at long last so is Andrew Flintoff."

Looking back, Flintoff too felt that things were clicking into place. "Throughout that year [2002], though I didn't do great, I thought I was getting better," he said. "After I missed the Australia trip, I came home, worked really hard and thought, well, I'm better than I was. I know my game better and I know what I need to do."

He may have blotted his copybook slightly with a boozy night out with Steve Harmison after the defeat by Australia for which he was fined, but he returned home, a hero of sorts, to Rachael and with a lucrative new bat contract with a manufacturer called Woodworm. The company was unknown – the idea had come when Mr Bob Sillett, 60, found an old bat rotted by woodworm in his garage in Billinghurst – and they needed something, someone, to get their name into the public domain. The managing director Joe, Bob's son, says: "When we wanted someone to promote the bats, there was no-one else we considered. It had to be Freddie – he was the one with the charisma."

They had just made a very wise investment.

Left: Australia knocked England out of the 2003 World Cup, but Flintoff was easily the most economical bowler in the tournament.

the**VAUGHAN**factor

Flintoff strode across the summer of 2003 a golden colossus, leaving perspiring bowlers at every step. His batting, for so long all promise and no delivery, finally flowered. He had learnt how to marry discipline and his own ox-throwing strength.

Fed up with the previous winter's shenanigans and the mental and physical grind of recovering from injury, he felt determined to throw himself into the year and not think about the past. "When I got back into the Test side in 2003 I made a conscious decision not to look back and to draw a line under everything that had gone before," he told *The Lancashire Evening Post*. "I said to myself – this is my Test career starting now."

Two other changes were vital to his melodious year. The first was that a new man was in charge of England. Nasser Hussain had been replaced as one day captain by Michael Vaughan, Flintoff's old A-team leader, after the World Cup. And it took only the first drawn Test against South Africa before Hussain decided that he could no longer stay on as captain of the Test side either.

So on 28 July, while chewing a bacon butty in the Edgbaston dressing room, Vaughan became England captain. It was a transition which helped Flintoff. Although he was very fond of Hussain, who had helped him develop from wastrel to cog of the team, he wasn't a fan of his authoritarian style; where Hussain had been a strict father figure, Vaughan preferred a more laissez-faire approach.

"Nasser was a lot more animated, ruled with more discipline and was more like a schoolteacher with us," Flintoff says in his autobiography. "He was a very passionate captain and very astute, but he did it with a style I didn't particularly like. He was confrontational and put a bit of undue pressure on the lads at times. He used to eff and jeff at mid-on and throw his cap around, but that's the way Nasser is.

"Vaughan likes me to play with a smile on my face. I don't think it any accident that I have played some of my best cricket under Michael simply because he encourages you to enjoy your cricket without fear of failure. I don't want to see my captain throwing his cap on the floor or kicking sods out of the ground."

So for Flintoff, Test cricket became a more relaxing environment. Meanwhile, back at Lancashire, he had been working with coach Mike Watkinson on his batting. Long days in March and April were filled with Watkinson bowling to Flintoff from 17 yards rather than 22, so that he could fine-tune his batting, speed up his reaction times and work on knowing where his off-stump was. And he would return to the exercise time after time. It seemed to work, too – confidence-building runs for Lancashire at the start of the season presaged a match-winning 98 for England at The Oval against South Africa at the end.

Of course, Flintoff being Flintoff, a season couldn't be a season without injury. He had been batting in the nets in May when he was struck on the arm by the fiery young Lancashire quick bowler Sajid Mahmood. A compressed nerve in the shoulder put him out of the Test series against Zimbabwe, though he did continue batting for Lancashire. His form was blistering and he finished the summer with two hundreds and two fifties in five championship matches at an average of 103.8 – teetering at the top of a Lancashire list in which Stuart Law and Carl Hooper also enjoyed prolific years.

**Chapter opener: New captain Michael Vaughan's less abrasive style of captaincy suited Flintoff.
Right: Goughie and Freddie celebrate another wicket during the 2003 Natwest Challenge.**

Sharing the dressing room with Hooper, the former West Indies batsman who had been one of his boyhood heroes, made the year even more of a thrill. "When he walked in I felt like that 17-year-old lad again," Flintoff said.

Because despite his England successes, he still loved, and loves, playing for Lancashire. He relishes the craic and the friendship. "The thing is you're playing with ten of your mates; it is really enjoyable, you turn up and everyone wants to do well," he said. "It is just unfortunate the way the international calendar is now that we can't play more. You might only pop in for two or three games a year, but they're trying to win a championship or a one-day trophy and you just want to help them out as best you can. I just like watching them – how sad am I? I really enjoy being in the dressing room and having a laugh to be honest."

His shoulder injury healed enough for him to start bowling again for Lancashire in early June and it took only 15 balls to conjure up a wicket against Middlesex with the Pakistani all-rounder Abdul Razzaq trapped on the back foot. Michael Vaughan was watching and happy to pencil a full-strength Flintoff into the one-day side.

Vaughan had created a team in his own image – young and resourceful. Flintoff suddenly found himself the third most capped player, and enjoyed the extra responsibility. He was batting at five and bowling first change. He even found himself giving the occasional team-talk in a huddle. After a low-key start in the three match one-day series against Pakistan, the fun began in the NatWest series with South Africa and Zimbabwe.

Flintoff made 53 in the first game against Zimbabwe, then a rapid 32 in the second against South Africa as well as taking three wickets. By the fifth, at Bristol, expectation had replaced hope. He had taken three for 13 to help ridicule Zimbabwe but England had slumped to 25 for four when he strode to the crease. Nine overs later he had sealed victory with a top-edged hook for six. "I think I'm at my best when I'm trying to hit the ball and being aggressive," he said afterwards. "He has been our linchpin player," said Vaughan as Flintoff squirmed

next to him in the press conference, embarrassed. England won the final at Lord's against South Africa on 12 July and all eyes swung to the Test series.

The first, which ended in a draw, was dominated by the young South African captain Graeme Smith's double century and Nasser Hussain's unexpected resignation. The second at Lord's, Michael Vaughan's first Test in charge, was grotty – defeat in four days by an innings, topped off by the new captain having to watch the South Africans dance the conga in celebration. Only one of his team got any praise from Vaughan in the post-match press conference – Andrew Flintoff. He had been out cheaply hooking in the first innings, but made a derring-do 142 in the second innings – which, if it meant nothing in the cause of the match, was to give him a priceless injection of confidence for the rest of the summer.

Flintoff's first Test hundred in England, and a record for an English No. 7 at Lord's, gave the crowd something to cherish and laugh out loud about, as the South African bowlers were splattered across the field. One ball was hit so hard that he cracked his great bat in half, and seemed, deliberately or not, to be sending a huge "V" sign back to the South Africans, as he held it up to the dressing room for a replacement.

The highlight was when Shaun Pollock, a bowler who visibly shrivels with every run conceded, was dispatched for 20 off an over. Jimmy Anderson, the No. 11, was holed up at one end, at the other Flintoff was on 118. The first ball went over long off for six, the second zipped through extra-cover for four. The third, a slower ball, was dispatched for four, as was the fourth – short and wide. The fifth was driven loftily for two. England were thrashed, but Flintoff had ensured that they went to Nottingham with a little bounce in their step.

But while the crowd basked in his hitting, Flintoff was bashful, even embarrassed. Statistics have just never meant that much to him, as he summarized afterwards. "I got a hundred but we got beat." His eye is always for the bigger picture. "I try and look at a season and see how many games I've influenced rather than averages."

Previous pages: The 2003 Natwest Trophy champions show off the trophy.
Left: The big-hitter cracks his bat on the way to his first Test hundred in England, August 2003.

His influence was to hum with intent through the rest of the series. An invaluable 30 during the victory at Trent Bridge, two fifties at Headingley batting with the tail (although he told *The Sunday Times*: "I got it wrong, I should have been more careful") and a match-winning, head-over-heels hoopla at The Oval. A 95 so ridiculous, it made the great stoic Graeme Smith lose his nerve; yet so vital it helped England win the match and draw the series. The watching crowd dared not move a finger.

A draw had looked inked in when England were eight wickets down but only 18 ahead of South Africa's first-innings score on the fourth morning. Then Flintoff walked out.

He hit 20 off the first 50 balls, 30 off the next 38 and 45 off the next 36 before trying to blast Paul Adams out of the big top with a second successive six and being bowled for 95.

Quick bowler Makhaya Ntini was dispatched for two massive sixes to the Pavilion End as the ball was punished with amazing power and, accompanied by another crack, one more Woodworm bat said a very public farewell. Yet Flintoff still had the nous to farm the strike – in a stand of 99 with Flintoff, Steve Harmison contributed three. Harmison, probably more talented at making the tea in the morning than with the bat, just stuck in there, determined to see his friend through to his hundred. Flintoff just loved it. "My adrenalin fed off the excitement generated by those excited noisy supporters."

The dazed South Africans crumbled in their second innings and Marcus Trescothick knocked off the runs practically single-handed. England had, incredibly, tied the series. South Africa named Flintoff Man of the Series, despite the amount of sledging they sent his way. It was a surprise for Flintoff. "I don't think that they think I'm very good," he said with a big smile on his broad face afterwards. "They question everything I do."

He ended the series averaging over 50 and with a growing and adoring following. Mike Selvey in *The Guardian* wrote: "Flintoff is the biggest crowd-pleaser to emerge here in two decades and a genuine international match-winner now."

There were still chinks – although Flintoff bowled the most overs of any England player, his ten wickets cost 59 apiece. Angus Fraser in *The Wisden Cricketer* said that Flintoff should "be hungrier for success and should expect more from himself and his fielders. And he needs to learn when to bang it in around the batsman's ribcage and when he would be better off bowling a fuller and more threatening length."

Flintoff himself said: "I'm still a bit of a novice with the ball, because with all the back problems I've never really had a chance to work at it. I'm trying to develop one that goes out when I need it to rather than just a fluke." And there was no doubt which of his two strings he preferred. In the autumn of 2003 he said: "Bowling is harder than batting. I remember speaking to Chris Cairns and he said bowling is the hard work, you just bat for fun, and that's pretty much the way it is to be honest. I hope I can be more successful, I've improved in 12 months and if I can improve in the next 12 I'll take more wickets."

His summer of success led England to give him a central contract for the first time in early September, meaning that he was under the full-time supervision of the ECB, and not Lancashire. England's improved pastoral care also extended to letting Flintoff miss the early-autumn Test series against Bangladesh because of a twinge in his groin that he had felt during the Oval Test – it seemed that Flintoff's superiors were also learning how to deal with their big all-rounder.

Flintoff did make a brief sojourn to Bangladesh for the one-day series. His tour started well when he captained England for the first time in a warm-up match in Dhaka – another sign of the English management's recognition of his increased maturity. Then the one-day series started and he proceeded to eat Bangladeshi bowlers for breakfast. He picked up the Man of the Match award in all three games – caned Bangladesh to all parts of the ground, made 177 runs, was never out, took seven for 63 and won the final game with a six. He passed Ian Botham's England record for sixes in one-day internationals. Botham hit 44 in 116 innings,

Flintoff matched him in just 64. He also shot up the Price Waterhouse Coopers ratings to be the world's leading all-rounder, overtaking South Africa's giant Jacques Kallis. The next stop on the first part of the winter tour was not likely to be such a breeze – England flew south to face Sri Lanka and an injury-free Muttiah Muralitharan.

Flintoff knew Murali from his Lancashire days. They were good friends, but as an opponent he would be formidable. "He's a brave cricketer, a lovely man," Murali said of Freddie. But he didn't like him well enough to bowl anything easy – he released his doosra, England were spellbound and Flintoff was out to him four times in three Tests. "He's a magician," said Flintoff afterwards.

As in India, Flintoff struggled against spin, and was averaging less that seven in Asia when at last he made 77 in the third Test. But it was a brave innings as he knuckled down, kicking away Muralitharan while attacking the others – though Murali got his man in the end. Flintoff pounded in with the ball, all heart, as he had in the previous two Tests. But England fell to pieces and lost by an innings and 215 runs – their third heaviest defeat in 127 years. The smiling Murali, who had allegedly been taunted by Nasser Hussain in the second Test, took 26 wickets in the series. England flew home disconsolate in time for Christmas, but Flintoff had built on his reputation again. *Wisden* wrote: "By the end of the year an England team without Flintoff in it seemed inconceivable."

England had two months to prepare for the Caribbean tour and they did it well – a sensational team performance brought the first series win in the West Indies since 1967–68 – ten years before Flintoff was born. For Flintoff it was a successful time too, finally, with the ball. To top that Rachael, now his fiancée, was carrying their first baby.

England took the series 3–0, with only Brian Lara stopping the rout at Antigua where he reclaimed Matthew Hayden's record for the highest Test innings with 400 not out. England's strength lay with their fearsome pace attack. Steve Harmison, Matthew Hoggard, Simon Jones and Flintoff proved ferocious and insatiable, and the West

Indian batting, fragile of confidence, just crumbled.

The Man of the Series award justly went to Harmison, whose 23 wickets at 14 included seven for 12 in the second innings of the first Test in Jamaica as six slips and a gully looked on hungrily. The West Indies were all out for 47 and Grievous Bodily Harmison, as *The Sun* dubbed him, had at last claimed the figures to prove his potential. He also cracked Flintoff's resolve not to have a drink on tour as raucous celebrations followed the win. When he took six for 61 in the second Test, Harmison had undeniably made it.

Flintoff's tour had started well when he stripped down to his sports kit and revealed that he was the fittest of the squad during the pre-tour exercises at the National Academy in Loughborough. It finished well too, with an unbeaten hundred in the fourth Test which ensured that England managed to draw Lara's match. It was a most unFlintoffian affair – he played with utmost caution, turned down easy singles to keep the strike and ignored the best and most provocative poses the West Indian bowlers could throw at him. It took him over five-and-a-half hours and was another step in his growing stature as a cricketer.

In between he had, at last, achieved his first five-wicket haul in Tests. In Barbados he was the one bowler who found the right length for the Bridgetown pitch and, despite the usual quota of dropped chances off his bowling, dismissed two of the danger men in Brian Lara and Shivnarine Chanderpaul. When he finally got his fifth man, as Fidel Edwards nudged the ball to Chris Read, even the poker-faced Duncan Fletcher managed a smile. Flintoff and his team-mates were chuffed to bits.

At the end of the series, Geoff Boycott, in the West Indies as a commentator, pronounced that the Flintoff who went home with a tour batting average of 50 and 11 wickets at 27 was now "a serious cricketer". He flew home to another accolade – he was named one of *Wisden*'s Five Cricketers of the Year for 2004, alongside two of the South Africans he had tormented in the previous summer – Graeme Smith and Gary Kirsten.

GOLDEN times

Smiling Flintoff, laughing Flintoff, gallant Flintoff, victorious Flintoff, daddy Flintoff... throughout the summer of 2004 the newspapers were dominated by pictures of one man's beaming face.

It had all seemed so unlikely in the late spring. After such a successful 12 months, surely Flintoff's form would have to plateau? But it didn't. He got better and better, until even the Australians started taking note. There were awards from on high – the International One-day Cricketer of the Year, and a place in the World One-day XI of the Year – and from his peers, who voted him the Players' Player of the Year. His personal life too was happy: his baby daughter Holly was born in September 2004, and he was to be married the following March.

It turned out that his century in Antigua was not just a sign of a new maturity but the start of an amazing run – it was followed by a score of over fifty in each of his next seven Tests. And as Flintoff grew in stature, so did England – winning eight Tests in a row stretching from the first Test against New Zealand at Lord's in May to the first against South Africa in Port Elizabeth just before Christmas, with the small matter of a whitewash of the West Indies in between. The two golden runs were not unconnected.

Flintoff playing well brought the team confidence, buzz, life. He had become what Mike Atherton had urged Michael Vaughan to make him when he took over the captaincy – the "central cog". And as the team got better, so did Flintoff's bowling figures. As the team were more successful, they grew in confidence, caught more of their chances and a famously unlucky bowler started getting luckier. And at the other end Steve Harmison had hit his stride, giving Flintoff more

bowling support. Meanwhile, an ankle injury which meant he was not able to bowl as many overs accidentally turned him from a stock bowler to a strike bowler.

The 2004 international season started in mid-May. Flintoff had returned home from the West Indies promising his fiancée that he would don his overalls and do some DIY – but with only two weeks between the final one-day international in Barbados and the first Test against New Zealand he did not have much time. The summer calendar was packed – three Tests against New Zealand, four against the West Indies, the NatWest series against West Indies and New Zealand, the NatWest Challenge against India and the ICC Champions Trophy.

For Flintoff, New Zealand were the *hors d'oeuvres*. A series expected to be tight ended in England's total victory because of an unlucky run of injuries for the tourists and England's growing spirit. Flintoff's biggest contribution was 94 in the second Test at Headingley when in partnership first with Graham Thorpe and then with the young wicket-keeper Geraint Jones (a precursor of what was to come) he helped take England to a substantial first-innings lead. It was particularly impressive because the bat wasn't feeling good in his hands that day: "The wicket was a bit up and down, and I had to really knuckle down because I didn't feel I was in great nick," he said.

Another fifty followed in the third Test at Trent Bridge before he was trapped lbw by Chris Cairns, New Zealand's own springy-haired charismatic all-rounder who had chosen to retire from Test cricket at his old home ground in Nottingham. Cairns' final flourish was nine wickets in the match and as he was stepping off the bottom rung of the

Chapter opener: Flintoff is thrilled to clean bowl Brian Lara during England's 4–0 series win over West Indies in summer 2004: Right: Howzat!

ladder, Flintoff was clambering towards the top.

At the end of June it was announced that Flintoff would miss the triangular one-day series with a small bony growth on the back of his left ankle that had been discovered during the Trent Bridge Test. The ECB doctors had prescribed two weeks' rest. But eight days later, Flintoff was miraculously back in the squad again, to play as a specialist batsman. The reason? Two horrible performances by England which left them in danger of being knocked out of their own competition. The contest to find someone who batted at No. 6, swallowed everything that came his way in the slips and bowled first change had ended without a winner. Michael Vaughan's brave words after defeat to New Zealand – "Flintoff's a key player, a world-class player, but we can't use it as an excuse for losing games. We can win games without Andrew Flintoff and we will win games without Andrew Flintoff" – blew like tumbleweed across the ground.

But what followed made it all worthwhile. Flintoff made two hundreds in three days. The first, against the West Indies, was the most welcome – his long-awaited maiden one day international century. But the second, against New Zealand, was the better innings. It included seven sixes – the most in a one-day innings by an Englishman. England still failed to make the final, but Flintoff had stoked the fires for the Test series against the West Indies to follow.

Light-hearted revenge over Tino Best was his first coup. At Port-of-Spain in March, Flintoff had been duped when he ducked from a ball that Best had only pretended to bowl. At Lord's, during England's 210-run first-Test win, Flintoff got his man. As Best came out to bat, Flintoff stage-whispered from slip, indicating to the Media Centre opposite: "Mind the windows, Tino." Best coltishly charged Ashley Giles, was stumped for three and Flintoff and his team-mates guffawed all the way to the victory podium.

Then, on 30 July, came a day that neither Flintoff, his father nor Brian Lara will forget – for very different reasons. Flintoff because the 167 he hit that day was his highest Test score, a galactic effort

including seven sixes – three off one over from Omari Banks; Lara because all he could do was stand forlorn at slip as his bowlers were flogged to all corners of the ground – his fears of what might be about to be unleashed clear when he greeted Flintoff's arrival at the crease by dispatching his fielders to guard the boundary ropes. Colin Flintoff's big moment came courtesy of one of those seven sixes, as a television audience of millions watched a ball from Jermaine Lawson soar high into the top tier of the Ryder Stand where a smiling, middle-aged man with a familiar face let it fall through his fingers. From a crowd of 19,500 people, Flintoff had managed to pick out his dad.

"His nickname at work was 'Colin Big-hands' and every weekend dad would come home telling us about the great catches he'd held," said Freddie. "But he fumbled the ball and it landed in Michael Vaughan's mum's lap sitting in the row behind. I burst out laughing when I saw where it had gone. I would have been the first batsman in Test history to have been caught by his dad." Colin Flintoff found himself replaying the moment for a photograph in *The Times*. "When you're sitting in the top deck of the stand you normally think you're safe, but Andrew is such a clean striker of the ball that you can't take your eyes off it for a second."

It had been a great innings, he had ignored the testing stuff and pummelled the rest like a waste-disposal man on a mission. And it was all done with a huge smile and a piratical ginger beard across his face. Flintoff's reaction afterwards? "Sometimes you just have to get your head down." He finished off his happy visit to Birmingham with the wickets of Ramnaresh Sarwan and Lara.

Two weeks later, mid-August, and Old Trafford was preparing for its day in the sun. And at Flintoff's home ground, Michael Vaughan was willing his star upwards. "Freddie is probably the best player in the world at the moment," he said. "The crowd will obviously go mad when he goes out to the wicket, but he's got to try and control his emotions. That's the progression of Freddie over the last year. A year or so ago he'd be the first to admit that when the crowd roared he'd try and hit

Left: A fired–up Flintoff adds Ramnaresh Sarwan to his list of victims, clean–bowling the West Indies number three during the third Test at Old Trafford, August 2004.

the first ball out of the ground for six, get 20-odd then get out. He's learned a hell of a lot."

Remarkably it was only Flintoff's second Test at Old Trafford, and he celebrated by extending his hoodoo over Lara, claiming his wicket in both innings, which made it three times in 20 balls. And the 57 he made in the second innings that August is still his highest Test score in Manchester. He was later to nominate walking off the Old Trafford pitch on the Monday afternoon with Robert Key as his favourite moment of the summer – a fifty in front of his home fans and a partnership with an old friend that won the series for England.

A three-day whipping of the West Indies at The Oval completed the rout, with 72 from Flintoff making it the eighth time in successive Tests that he had made 50 or more, something only done by one other No. 6 in history, Sir Gary Sobers.

"Flintoff imposes himself by his stature," Andrew Hall of South Africa had observed the previous summer. "It is part of his game plan, he likes to have that edge and physical presence." The West Indies seemed to be shrinking from it much as England had all but turned tail when Viv Richards used to swagger out to the crease.

When Fidel Edwards was yorked by Jimmy Anderson to bowl out the West Indies for the last time, and England needed only four to win, Flintoff bear-hugged each of his colleagues in turn, in sheer delight. During the Old Trafford Test, a young substitute fielder, Alastair Bressington, had dropped Chris Gayle and looked desperate. When later, at third man, he held on to a skier, it was Flintoff who got to him first, running 80 yards to envelop him. It all added to the impression of a man for whom kindness was a way of life. He was Man of the Series in more than one way.

It was Paul Coupar of *Wisden* who found the words to describe Flintoff's glorious unselfishness and joy in other people's achievement, quoting GK Chesterton, he wrote: "There is a great man who makes every man feel small. But the real great man is the man who makes every man feel great."

Flintoff's rapport with his team-mates was equalled only by his rapport with the crowd. Like an old-fashioned politician standing on a soap box, he fed off their applause. During his 99 in the second match of the one-day series against India, the game seemed powered by a *joie de vivre*. When Flintoff was out for 99 there was no scowl at missing out, just a big fat grin.

And his summer was about to get even better with the birth of his daughter Holly on 6 September. He was the second England player to become a father that summer after Michael Vaughan in June. Holly arrived a month early, in London, and neither he nor Rachael had even a babygrow with them. So, in his capacity as agent, Neil Fairbrother had to drive down from Cheshire in their family car loaded with the necessary, and then drive their child-unfriendly two-seater back up again. The day after the birth was the ICC awards dinner and a very happy Flintoff won the One-day Player of the Year. The photographs caught him afterwards, tie askew, hair ruffled, tanked-up eyes, dopey grin.

In his absence, England had lost their third match against India. The Indian captain, Sourav Ganguly – not Flintoff's soul-mate by any means – said: "England are a far different side without him."

There was just one more tournament before the English season finished its longest ever run. The ICC Champions Trophy – a 12-country competition held in England in September. There were moans about the weather, the early dusk, the dew, the light, the marketing, the mismatches – but Flintoff provided some theatre with a scintillating hundred against Sri Lanka at The Rose Bowl on a pitch that helped the bowlers. Again he played himself in, again he later exploded – the first 50 runs came off 69 balls, the second 50 off just 20 as he blasted England into the semi-finals. Only 6,000 had turned up to watch a game that was forced to go into the second day because of rain, but those who did were rewarded. "It was the perfectly paced one-day innings," said Vaughan afterwards. In six one-day outings, separated by the West Indies Test series, Flintoff had made three centuries and a 99.

England's opponents for the semi-final were Australia. A country groaned, but England won by

Right: A stylish follow-through, but Flintoff claimed he got too bogged down with batting technique during the 2004–05 South Africa tour.

six happy wickets on a bitterly cold day. Australia's coach John Buchanan said it was "no more than a snapshot in time." The spectators who saw England's first one-day win over Australia for 14 games were rather more excited. That was the highlight of the tournament for England, who went on to lose to the West Indies in the final – a nail-biter in which Flintoff took three wickets, including Lara's for the umpteenth and last time that summer, but the tail wagged improbably to steer the West Indies home.

All this time the Australian leg-spinner Shane Warne had been watching carefully, both from Australia and from Hampshire where he was captain. He told *The Times*: "He gets the odd break because of his confidence and self-belief. It is no coincidence. Players who change games are the ones who back themselves and have an aura that sends signals to the opposition."

England were going to Zimbabwe at the end of November, but Flintoff wasn't. He had seen a Channel 4 documentary about Zimbabwe while recuperating from injury before the 2003 World Cup and had made up his mind that he did not want to go. Things hadn't changed, and he and Steve Harmison decided in mid-summer that, for moral reasons, they would not tour. So there was some time at last to spend with his new daughter.

"Everything has gone my way with England in 2004, but I've had to work harder than I've ever done in my life. I have a greater awareness of what's needed to compete and survive at Test level," he told the *Lancashire Evening Post*, in November. "People who know me realize I haven't changed that much. Loyalty is very important to me and I'll never forget where I've come from."

Flintoff trained at Oliver's boxing gym in Salford, where he endured the toughest exercise regime of his life. He flew to South Africa for an intense tour (five Tests in six weeks with no non-internationals once the series had started) fit, but in poor form with the bat. His confidence didn't improve even when he was voted third, behind Britain's Olympic heroes Kelly Holmes and Matthew Pinsent, in the BBC's Sports Personality of the Year award. The

Peter Kay "Coming in your ears" Chorley FM T-shirt he sported for the video-link may have won him a few late votes.

He later told *The Independent on Sunday* that he had just got too bogged down technically with his batting on that tour: "I am not just a one-dimensional player, but I think that in South Africa I got too wrapped up with trying to play the perfect innings rather than just playing the way I play."

The series was tough, and England didn't play pretty, but they won and ended the year the only Test team undefeated in 2004. Flintoff emerged from his sticky patch with the bat in the final Test to make 77 – his slowest Test fifty. But he bowled and bowled and bowled – taking his 100th Test wicket in the third Test at Cape Town. As *Wisden* wrote: "The toll on Flintoff's mighty body was enormous... he was always the bowler to whom Vaughan turned when he wanted control and to slow the scoring, so much so that he over-bowled him at times."

By the end of the series, which England took 2–1, Flintoff's ankle was hurting again, with the same complaint as the previous summer. There was talk of having more injections and playing through the pain, but both Flintoff and Vaughan decided that this was not the right approach. He would fly home, have the operation and try to get fit for the Ashes. The biggest year of Flintoff's cricketing life was to begin, as so many others had, with an operation and the struggle to get fit.

On the other side of the world, people were watching his progress. In mid-summer of 2004, Stuart Law, the Queenslander who became a team-mate of Flintoff's at Lancashire spoke to an Australian newspaper about the search for the new Botham. "They [the English] are always on the search, now you've got a kid who is probably just as good if not better than Ian Botham and he's just taken the world by storm. He's six-foot-four and 16 stone, so he's got absolutely no fear whatsoever. I think the Australians should stand up and take notice of this guy, because if anyone's going to destroy them..." Law tailed off. He turned out to be a good judge.

Previous pages: Freddie and fans hail a 2–1 series win following the drawn final Test in South Africa, January 2005; Right: Michael Vaughan and "the best player in the world at the moment."

bring on the
AUSSIES

Everything boiled down to this – Thursday morning, 21 July 2005, Lord's. Long queues had been in place since 3pm the previous afternoon, curious clouds hung stubbornly in the sky, cameras were everywhere. The atmosphere at the famous old ground, often mocked for having all the buzz of the British Library, was approaching electric.

It is Andrew Flintoff's first Ashes Test. Ricky Ponting wins the toss and England are bowling. At 10.25am, Flintoff and the rest of the team clump over the rubberized floor of the Long Room, their boots sounding louder than thunder. A whoosh of released anticipation blasts their ears as they walk onto the field.

From the start it is all England, all Steve Harmison. Justin Langer plays and misses at the first ball and is hit on the elbow by the second. Matthew Hayden and Ponting require treatment, too – Harmison striking Ponting on the grill of his helmet in the 11th over and drawing first blood, which drips down the Australian captain's face and on to his shirt. It is sustained, thrilling fast bowling from the Pavilion End.

And when Harmison rests, Flintoff comes on – and immediately breaks through. Langer can't resist a short one, pulls and is gone. England end the morning session with an eight-man slip cordon, and leave for lunch to a standing ovation. Australia are 97 for five.

Inevitably, Flintoff's build-up to this moment had been anything but straightforward. He flew back from South Africa, saw a specialist about his latest ankle problem, and was hurried into the operating theatre. The surgery, to remove a bone spur on his left ankle, had a recovery period of three or four months and before long he was back in the safe hands of Dave Roberts.

They devised a fitness campaign and, by early February, Flintoff was hobbling on crutches at Cartmel races to watch his horse run, and telling the press that he would be fit for the Ashes. He had another, equally important engagement, rather sooner than that – his wedding day on 5 March. "And the groom wore crutches" was not quite the image he had envisaged.

In late February, Flintoff and 55 friends flew to Budapest for his stag weekend. Flintoff wore a bootcast and came back minus a mobile phone – thought to be starting a long journey down the Danube – and a strip of hair around the centre of his head. "As you can imagine my wife Rachael was over the moon – the wedding pictures are great," he said.

Inevitably he had to shave his head completely for the wedding, which took place a week or so later in London. Rachael wore a full white dress and Flintoff a suit, and the day went like a dream. They had turned down offers from magazines for a *Hello*-style wedding, but the very fact that there was that opportunity was proof of Flintoff's growing public profile – cricketers don't usually feature alongside minor European royalty and the cast of *Hollyoaks*.

There was no honeymoon. Flintoff's training schedule was tight and no time could be spared. "It [his rehabilitation] is very comprehensive," Neil Fairbrother explained. "They'll give him a day off to get married, but there's no time for a honeymoon. They'll have to make up for that later."

So it was back to the endless grind – hydrotherapy at Blackburn Football Club, the gym, nets and long runs, all with the aim of being fit to play at the start of the season. It could be a tiring and frustrating experience, especially for someone not in love with

Chapter opener: Paying attention to England coach Duncan Fletcher during the Ashes build-up; Right: Freddie and friends are suited and booted for his wedding day.

physical jerks. But Flintoff being Flintoff, he still found the time to be the star guest for a fund-raising dinner at Whittingham and Goosnargh, his dad's cricket club, in early April. The event was a sell-out – Flintoff took questions from the floor and Sir Tom Finney, Preston's famous footballing son, wished him luck.

Soon afterwards, there was time to shake away some of the cobwebs of frustration in a practice match between the Lancashire players at Old Trafford where he crashed 119 from 99 balls. Such was the level of interest in Flintoff's Ashes prospects that the Lancashire manager Mike Watkinson was asked for a statement on an internal warm-up match. "Freddie's playing purely as a specialist batsman," he said. "He won't be bowling or fielding, he was only jogging between the wickets."

Flintoff played his first match of the season at Lord's on 24 April, and the press box was packed. A spring National League match had rarely seen such a buzz. Flintoff came in, flexed an extra-cover drive and was out for 17. Nothing for the hardy spectators to get excited about, but satisfactory – the ankle was fine. So the press circus moved on to New Road where Lancashire were playing Worcestershire in their second championship game of the season and Flintoff made a fifth-ball nought in the first innings. He was finding all the attention overbearing. "I even ended up doing a press conference after I got my duck… It was on the front page if I blew my nose," he wrote in *Being Freddie*.

The build-up to all this had started when England were away in South Africa during the winter, when the team's results were discussed not so much in terms of the series being played, but what they meant in the context of the Ashes.

At home the anticipation simply grew. The first University games had just been played on frosty ground, and England had two Tests against Bangladesh, then two one-day international competitions before the Ashes started. But already Ashes fever, and Flintoff fever, was building.

His progress was watched by international journalists who normally don't see a ball of county cricket; down in Hampshire, Kevin Pietersen, the young South African batsman who had qualified for England and taken the one-day series in his home country by storm, was in a similar goldfish bowl. The five grounds holding Ashes Tests had completely sold out for the first four days months in advance – and at The Oval all the tickets for all five days were sold long before the Australians had even arrived.

Flintoff's last proper county workout before Bangladesh arrived was at Old Trafford where he was to meet Steve Harmison, this time 22 yards away and wearing a Durham shirt. Harmison came away the winner. Flintoff had made a 53-ball half-century before Steve Garratt, umpiring his second championship match, adjudged him lbw to Harmison, despite his forward defensive push. Flintoff was as crestfallen as Harmison was laughingly exuberant, but he had managed to bowl a handful of overs in the game.

Poor Bangladesh arrived to a fairly underwhelming welcome. Most people were impatient for the Ashes to start and had little interest in a team who had won only one Test, against Zimbabwe. True to form, they were thrashed, comprehensively, in their two-Test series. Flintoff did not get a chance to see how he felt at the crease – he wasn't needed to bat.

He had at least had a chance to bowl – finishing with nine wickets at 15.33 – and his action had provoked the interest of Peter Roebuck, the ex-Somerset captain turned journalist, who had been watching on television. He claimed in *The Sydney Morning Herald* that Flintoff was a chucker. Flintoff's final spell at Lord's against Bangladesh "contained some of the most blatant transgressions of the law covering legitimate actions seen in respectable company this year," wrote Roebuck. "Flintoff's action seems to deteriorate when he searches for an extra yard of pace and especially when he moves around the wicket and starts to pound the middle of the pitch." Michael Vaughan dismissed the accusations and Dav Whatmore, Flintoff's former Lancashire coach who was now in charge of Bangladesh, had "no complaints".

Previous pages: Lashing out at the stumps after dropping a catch in practice; Right: Freddie gives Brett Lee a taste of things to come during England's Twenty20 thrashing of Australia.

Far more interesting than all that, the Aussies were here. They arrived on 5 June in a cavalcade of confidence. "I'm not looking at it as being the first to lose them [the Ashes]," said captain Ponting. "I'm looking at being another Australian captain to retain the Ashes. It comes back to us being here and preparing well."

Bill Brown, Australia's oldest living Test player, claimed that the Australians should be emulating the Invincibles of 1948 and remain unbeaten for the tour. Meanwhile, Shane Warne, who was not a member of the one-day team and had therefore not yet joined the squad, was maintaining his usual low profile by having his portrait unveiled in the Long Room at Lord's. The portrait by Fanny Rush made headlines when the artist claimed she had had to make Warne's groin smaller so as not to offend MCC members.

The war of words started immediately. Ponting let slip that Andrew Flintoff might just get into the Australian side. When Vaughan was asked which Australians would get into his, he replied "none".

The first meeting of the two sides, and the end of the phoney war was at the Rose Bowl for the inaugural international Twenty20 game. England hit the ground fizzing, and Flintoff dug the ball in short to the Australian tailenders. He hit Brett Lee on the helmet. It was the start of an epic battle between Lee and Flintoff. Australia were bowled out for 79, with their top seven batsmen falling for eight runs in 20 balls. England had won by a round 100 runs.

The newspapers had a field day. Mike Walters in *The Mirror* wrote: "To describe Australia's four-man pace attack as pie-throwers at such an early stage of their tour would be premature, but Messrs Pukka, Kipling, Bentos and Ginster could scarcely have fared any worse. In the field, the Aussies were no more accomplished, fumbling more than teens in the back row of your local cinema on a Saturday night." But the two captains rose above the hype. "A bit of a laugh," said Ponting; "a bit of a lottery," said Vaughan.

The England coach Duncan Fletcher, not an enthusiast by nature, was secretly jumping up and down in glee. "The most excited I got was after the Twenty20," he later admitted. "I had been impressed by our Champions Trophy win… but we needed that reaffirmed somehow, another win. The aggression was the part I liked when we went into that match. We got into their faces, got into their space and it was so well done – it was 'we can win this.'"

When Australia went on to lose to Somerset in a one-day match, despite knocking up 342, and were then beaten by the cricketing chumps of Bangladesh by five wickets in the first game of the NatWest Series, the country could hardly believe what they were seeing. The tourists became even more of a laughing stock when the Australian press officer revealed that the team had been spooked by ghosts at Lumley Castle, now a luxury hotel in Durham, where they had chosen to stay. Young all-rounder Shane Watson was so scared that he opted to spend the night on Brett Lee's floor. The Australian papers were choking. "What's worse than a whingeing Englishman?" screamed *The Sydney Daily Telegraph*. "Gloating Pommies". "One day we'll lose the Ashes," the paper continued, "and it will be as horrific as waking up after a night on the drink in a room full of images of Camilla Parker Bowles."

England meanwhile were just watching and waiting open-mouthed – though they knew from experience that this was unlikely to be the Australia that they would meet in the Ashes series. Their next game against Australia was at Bristol in the one day series. Flintoff played his part, as a foil to the firing Harmison, in dismissing the Aussies for 252, but England were heading for defeat until Kevin Pietersen smashed eight fours and four sixes in an unbeaten 91 to turn the game on its head. The watching Flintoff was impressed. "He really is some player," he wrote in his autobiography. "Very special."

The balance of power in world cricket then started to regain its equilibrium – with both sides beating Bangladesh and Australia beating England. Flintoff's batting was still stuck in first gear, as he kept lofting catches to long off or long on. The

Left: Adam Gilchrist got used to this feeling during the summer of 2005 as Flintoff dominated the normally destructive wicket-keeper/batsman.

final of the competition at Lord's ended in a tie, with Flintoff the pick of the bowlers with three wickets – including Adam Gilchrist, who was to become his trophy victim of the summer.

The NatWest Challenge didn't prove such a nail-biting contest, though. Australia won the three-match series 2–1, with their batsmen setting off a sudden avalanche of runs. There was some succour for Flintoff as he hit 87 in the second match, his highest score against Australia, and a relief for many who had been waiting for a promising pre-Ashes sign. It had been a mature innings; he had given himself time to feel secure at the crease before taking the attack to their bowlers. His bowling too was hitting all the right bits on the pinball machine, and without any pain from the ankle. He cut a formidable figure on the field – a giant of a man, hurling thunderbolts at speeds consistently over 90mph. He had put on weight, but not through too many late-night wrestles with a chicken masala: this was through strength training in the gym. He was, he wrote later, starting "to settle in and find the rhythm. I felt I got better and better during the [one-day] series and it was perfect timing for me for the Tests."

The countdown was on at last. All talk was of the Ashes. Players' thoughts on the upcoming series dominated interviews. Flintoff spoke to *The Independent on Sunday* in late July. "It's a big ask to get everything [batting and bowling] going together, but I would settle for doing it in the next seven or eight weeks."

The fact that this was his first Ashes series kept coming up – as if tattooed on his forehead. "I'd be lying if I said I hadn't had one eye on it, with the interest from the man in the street – the bog standard question, 'Are we going to do 'em then?' Because I have never played in one, this [series] is going to be extra special, and irrespective of what I have done in the game so far, come September I will be judged on how I've done this summer, and so will the team and everybody in it. I'm slightly nervous, but it is excitement more than nerves. I want to play in it, it's all you think about when you are younger. You want to play in an Ashes series

and a World Cup final." And to *The Sunday Times* he admitted: "If we do it [win the Ashes], it will probably be a life-changing moment for all of us."

Meanwhile Glenn McGrath announced that Australia would win 5–0 and their former bowler Rodney Hogg predicted that Flintoff would be "found out technically" by Shane Warne. There were also whispers from the Australian camp that Flintoff couldn't play fast bowling. Most experts, including Harbhajan Singh, who had experience of a series victory over Australia, were plumping for the tourists. "They play better in pressure situations," said Harbhajan.

England had not won an Ashes series since Mike Gatting's victorious tour of 1986–87. And they had not beaten the Aussies at Lord's, the venue for the first Test, since 1934.

On the Tuesday before the Test, Flintoff prepared with some comfort food – fish and chips with Ashley Giles and Steve Harmison. So wild was the build-up that by the time the game started the players were ready to explode. The number one side in the world, against the number two side in the world. This was it: the Ashes.

The England players lunched euphorically that first day. And, for a while, things only got better. Six overs into the afternoon session, Flintoff had his man again – Adam Gilchrist. Flintoff wrote in *Being Freddie* that they had a plan for Gilchrist, bowling from around the wicket and "putting it outside off-stump". After carving away a few times, Gilchrist capitulated, went for the big drive and was caught behind. Flintoff looked as if his eyes would pop out of his head. From there Warne and Simon Katich stuck around, but England had done the hard work and Australia were all out for 190 in just over 40 overs, just before tea. If they could have done, the crowd would have leapt from the stands and carried the team from the field on velvet divans – instead they made do with giving them their third standing ovation of the day.

But that was England's highpoint of the match. Not long after tea, their reply was in tatters at 21 for five, with Glenn McGrath taking all the wickets for two runs in 31 balls. Flintoff walked out to

Left: England's plan to stifle Adam Gilchrist by bowling around the wicket succeeds as Freddie induces a catch to Geraint Jones in the first innings of the First Test at Lord's.

an ovation – and back to a suffocating sigh of disappointment, bowled by McGrath's fast shooter for a duck. When he returned to the dressing room, he shouted: "I've just waited six years for that." By the close 17 wickets had fallen in the day, but Australia were on top.

Outside the rarified four walls of Lord's, more serious things were afoot – attempted bombings of the London transport system for the second time in a fortnight. No bombs were detonated, but some of the joy of the day disappeared as the lucky escape began to sink in.

That tumultuous day apart, the Test reverted depressingly to Ashes type. England were outplayed and, despite two half centuries from Pietersen, Australia won by 239 runs on the fourth day. McGrath was given his third Man of the Match award in three Tests at Lord's. Flintoff avoided a pair in the second innings, but tried to cut a slider from Shane Warne and was caught behind for three. He had taken four wickets for 173. He drove down to Devon for a two-day break to get away from it all with Rachael and Holly. He regarded his Ashes debut as "a shocker", describing the four days that had just passed as "a devastating match to play in."

Down in Devon's green pastures, Flintoff tried to switch off. "I realized that my best plan was to stick to what I had been doing for the past couple of years, to play with enjoyment and no fear of failure," he later told *The Times*.

But the speculation continued in his absence. Should Flintoff move down the order? Was he a good enough batsman against Australia to bat at six? How were England going to combat McGrath and Warne? Would Geraint Jones, the wicket-keeper who had a rotten time at Lord's, retain his place? Should Graham Thorpe have played? Was English cricket going to let this golden opportunity, a mood of great optimism and excitement, a summer without any big football tournaments or Olympics to cause a distraction, fall through its finger tips?

Flintoff came back home, had a few net sessions with Neil Fairbrother, scored some reassuring runs on Twenty20 finals day, and was introduced to a "mental coach" called Jamie Edwards, who had worked with two of Chubby Chandler's golf clients, Lee Westwood and Darren Clarke.

"They [Fairbrother and Chandler] asked me whether I'd have a chat with Fred before the next Test because he hadn't been entirely happy with himself," Edwards told the *Manchester Evening News*. "And Fred bought me in straight away. I think it helped us connect that I had played sport at a high level as well. But it's not woo-woo stuff I'm telling him. It's practical stuff in a language he can understand… Fred doesn't want to know the mechanics of how his brain works. He wants to press a button on a remote control to get the best out of himself. Now he knows how to do it. But at the end of the day, when he goes home and puts his key in the door he can go from being Freddie Flintoff to Andrew Flintoff." Unbeknown to Flintoff, Michael Vaughan had a similar session with one of Edwards' colleagues.

Flintoff hoped that he had got his groove back. He certainly talked the talk in his column in *The Sun* newspaper. "There's no panic in the England team – we still have good players. The rest of the series now is about our mental ability and strength of character as much as our technical skills. But the brilliant spirit in the squad has been built up over several years and one poor result has not changed anything. There are four Tests to go, that is a lot of cricket to be played over the next six weeks. We must come back strongly at Edgbaston next week."

And Australia themselves had had a scare. "They hit us as hard in the first couple of hours of the Lord's Test as we've been hit in recent years," Adam Gilchrist admitted later in the summer. "Although the result went the way it did, they made a pretty strong statement with the artillery they had and the way they used it. That game was much more even than the result showed."

Edgbaston was a ground where England had a good record. So good that many had called for the first Test to be played there. But this year it hosted the second match, and England's last chance to grab the skein of cotton that would pull them up from a pit of despair.

Left: "I've just waited six years for that… " A fast shooter from Glenn McGrath does for Flintoff in his first Ashes innings as Australia take a 1–0 series lead.

GIANT
amongst men

They say it was the greatest Test, of the greatest series of all. Edgbaston 2005: victory by a two-run margin, a hair's breadth so thin it was barely there, which hauled England back into the Ashes. Two runs made the difference between equality and conceding the series to Australia – nobody believed there could be a resurrection from 2–0 down. Even Michael Vaughan. "No way back from that," admitted the captain.

It was also Flintoff's Test – he rose like Poseidon from the Birmingham puddles and threw himself at Australia – the dominant force in a game that seemed at times to be controlled by the whims of the gods.

England's spirits had been lifted before the start when Glenn McGrath, their destroyer at Lord's and the bearer of 500 Test wickets, slipped during practice, twisted his ankle and finished up with ligament tears. He had to be carted off the field on a groundsman's buggy and would not bowl a ball. Never had a game of touch rugby been so important. England sat in the dressing room pumped up by what Flintoff called a "massive boost". Smiles broadened further when Ricky Ponting won the toss and decided to bowl on an Edgbaston pancake.

England had spent the previous week licking their wounds, but as the openers Andrew Strauss and Marcus Trescothick emerged they were given a standing ovation, and seemed to grow metres in stature. Trescothick blasted three fours off Brett Lee's second over – all through the covers, the third with an almighty thud. And that was the way it continued for the rest of the day – five an over, frenetic, hectic madness. When 132 runs came in the first session, the chairman of the English selectors David Graveney was so blown away that

he felt a Rubicon had been crossed – England would win the series.

Flintoff had been watching the openers blast away from the dressing room, quietly confident after a good session in the nets. It seemed for a while that he would be able to spend the day with his feet up, but a mid-order wobble meant that he was in after lunch. The man at the other end was Kevin Pietersen – this was the partnership the papers had been waiting for all summer, the double-act dubbed, in anticipation, the TNT twins.

Flintoff was on nought, facing Shane Warne, and full of doubt. He later told Simon Hughes of *The Daily Telegraph* what he was thinking. "Warne lobbed one up and I thought I'm going to hit it, then I thought 'should I, shouldn't I?' and it just cleared mid-off. I decided from that point that I wasn't going to die wondering, that I had to be positive." So he attempted to hit himself back into form – six fours and five tumultuous sixes followed in his 68 – one struck against Brett Lee seemed to be played with his eyes wide shut. He and Pietersen put on 103, with Pietersen playing second fiddle.

"It was good to watch," said Pietersen. "We're mature players, it's just a case of adapting. It would have been stupid for me to try to out-hit him and get out. I thought we played off each other real well."

England clobbered 407 runs in the day. The second was England's too, just. The Australians scored at the same frenetic pace of Thursday, but lost wickets more regularly and finished 99 behind. Flintoff had bowled well and he and Simon Jones together had started to reverse-swing the ball from early on. It was a nice surprise for Flintoff, who had learnt the art from Wasim Akram at Lancashire, but did not find it easy. But England's advantage seemed fragile when, in the evening,

Chapter opener: Flintoff is mobbed after bowling Simon Katich in the third Ashes Test.
Right: Launching one of a record nine sixes, this time off Shane Warne, during the second Test.

Shane Warne walked his walk from the City End and in his first and the last over of the day, bowled Andrew Strauss.

Things got worse mid-Saturday morning, with England 72 for five and defeat sticking her tongue out at the other end. But in strode Flintoff – and this was his day. He was at once circumspect and clever – by necessity for a while after putting his shoulder out while in single figures. "The other lads gave me some stick for making a fuss and being a bit of a Jessie," he later said. "I thought my arm was going to drop off." So he played pat-a-cake with the ball, ignoring the obvious temptations put in his way.

It was only when England were in the sink at 131 for nine, with Simon Jones at the other end, that he unleashed the trident. Kasprowicz bowled the next over – 20 came off it, including two soaring sixes. He didn't bowl another. Then came Lee – six, four, six, as Flintoff noted the nine fielders lining the boundary ropes, and ignored them. That made it nine sixes for the match – a record for an Ashes Test.

With Australia 47 for 0 needing 282, Michael Vaughan threw the ball to Flintoff. "We need a wicket or two," the captain deadpanned. And from that came the over of a career: the second ball got rid of Langer; the seventh, because of an earlier no-ball, was an outswinger to scalp Ricky Ponting for a duck; he'd been unsettled by two hearty lbw shouts in between.

"That's probably the best first over I've ever bowled," Flintoff said afterwards. "I was slightly fortunate to get Justin, as it hit his arm and his thigh – but to Ricky the first four balls were reverse-swinging, and I thought I'll just swap it round here, and it went! It was great.

"It's great when both parts of my game come together in the same match," he continued. "It doesn't happen very often."

Shane Warne paid tribute for Australia. "He was fantastic. He's a guy anyone would want in their side, the go-to man for England. Some of those drives off the back shoe off Brett ... amazing."

Australia were reeling at 175 for eight at the close, and the game should have been over quickly on Sunday morning. But it still had one more snaking twist up its sleeve as Warne, Lee and Michael Kasprowicz stubbornly stood in the way. With 62 needed, Flintoff bowled one full and long and Warne trod on his stumps. It should have been over, but Lee and Kasprowicz battled on – somehow resisting the ferocious Flintoff and Steve Harmison. Lee was hit on the hand and the arm and the body, but just picked up his bat and kept going. Simon Jones dropped a difficult chance at third man with 14 needed and Flintoff and Marcus Trescothick were standing at slip saying to each other: "They can't get this, can they?" Suddenly, with only three more needed, and nobody daring to look, Harmison's short ball found a leg-side tickle from Kasprowicz, and Geraint Jones held on. The crowd went absolutely crazy.

But while his team-mates celebrated around him, Flintoff went straight to Lee, who was crouched on the ground in exhaustion and despair. "You were unbelievable," he said. It was a selfless gesture, natural to the core, and a snapshot in time which will be used one hundred years on as an example of what sporting combat should represent. It was immediately compared to the picture of Bobby Moore and Pele embracing during the 1970 World Cup.

Flintoff, Man of the Match, of course, later hailed his fellow gladiator Lee. "I tried to bowl him out," he said, "and I tried to knock him out. I tried everything but he just kept coming back. He can be proud of what he did. He bowled great and he batted outstandingly. He is a champion."

There was little rest before the next Test, at Old Trafford, starting on the Thursday. It was Flintoff's 50th and he was desperate to do well on his home ground. He made 46, before being caught off Warne, but Michael Vaughan had rediscovered his golden touch, making 166 and steering England to a solid 444 – though not without Shane Warne picking up his 600th wicket. Australia looked as if they were going to fall short of the follow-on target, but crept past it thanks to 90 from Warne, whom almost everyone, England apart, wanted to make his maiden Test century. England batted

Previous pages: "We love you, Freddie, we do..." Flintoff mania reaches Bedrock.
Left: Giving Michael Vaughan a big lift after the heart-stopping second Test win.

105

again, and Andrew Strauss – who had been struggling both for form and against Warne – made a brave century, leaving Australia 423 to win, and England a day to bowl them out.

From eight o'clock the next morning, radio stations were telling people not to go to Old Trafford. The monster queue was winding its way down the Great Stone Road – children, mothers, grandfathers, babies, picnics, bicycles, walkmans, cigarettes in a babble of excitement. The police were at Manchester Piccadilly railway station, preventing people from getting on the tram; roads were closed around the ground – it was total chaos. Twenty thousand people had to be turned away at the gate, including young children in floods of tears. The players could not believe what they were seeing.

Nor could the spectators, the majority of whom watched every ball of the day, until the very last when the big screen at the ground exclaimed "One Ball, One Wicket". Ricky Ponting's century had taken Australia almost to the finish line, and somehow, with their innate ability to never give up, Brett Lee, again, and Glenn McGrath were there at the end. They had survived 24 balls of Flintoff and Harmison and an all-standing, all-baying crowd.

Flintoff had bowled until his legs were practically broken – 25 overs, the most he had ever sent down in a day. As he explained in his autobiography, he even had to change his action because his arms were so tired. He took four wickets, reverse-swinging it at speed, including Adam Gilchrist and Simon Katich in a mid-afternoon charge and, at exactly six o'clock, with the crowd beginning to despair, he took the wicket of Shane Warne – caught by Geraint Jones from a ball which rebounded of Andrew Strauss' upper thigh – to break a stand of 74 with Ponting. He celebrated with a backflip. The 7.7 million watching on Channel 4 and the 17,000 in the crowd did mental backflips of their own. But it wasn't quite enough.

Eleven England faces told one story – complete disappointment. But there was something to cling on to: that the Australians were celebrating a draw with the jubilation of a win. Ponting, Man of the Match for his innings born of stubborn brilliance,

summed up Flintoff afterwards. "He moves it both ways probably as much as anyone in the game and he does it at 90mph."

That evening, Flintoff was found not in the nearest bar with bright lights and a pounding bass, but in the hut with the mowers and the mops with the Lancashire groundsman Pete Marron – the man who had bought Flintoff his first drink many moons earlier.

Flintoff was physically and mentally exhausted, but there was some breathing space before the next Test. He flew to the French Riviera with Rachael and Holly – a refuge where cricket was not a national dish. Only one person broke the anonymous bliss – a man in a Preston North End shirt. And if Flintoff was feeling the strain, he certainly wasn't showing it. Paul Beck, a Lancashire cricket club sponsor and friend, and his family holidayed with him. "He's not flash," Beck said of Flintoff. "In France, we'd go out for lunch, spend four or five hours on the beach, swim and spend every evening chatting over a bottle of rosé. He's one of the most laid-back individuals I've met in my life. He's a very normal, rounded human being."

Back home Flintoff was now recognized everywhere he went – "Not just the blokes but women and teenagers as well," he said. Ashes fever was everywhere, football was disappearing from the back page and being pushed down the sports bulletins and England cricket shirts started outselling football strips. *The Times* reported a 20 percent increase in the sales of tea, scones and cucumber. On 22 August, *The Daily Telegraph* even had a headline: "Now Flintoff bends it like Beckham." It got to the stage where the life-size cut-out of Flintoff standing near the bar of his old club St Anne's was going to be asked for an opinion.

And there was no hiding from the public glare at Trent Bridge, as the next "Greatest Test" unfolded. Flintoff, again, dominated the match. His first Test century against Australia was a work of art. No caveman batting this.

"The innings of his life," said Geoff Boycott. "He was batting in a tough situation, but he had the mental pressure to deal with it as well as Australia's

Right: Another left-hander bites the dust... Australian opener Matthew Hayden falls victim to Flintoff's bowling on the final day of the drawn third Test.

bowlers. He curtailed his game and played with control, responsibility and great skill."

The headline in the *Melbourne Herald Sun* read simply, "Somebody stop him".

Flintoff was phenomenal, and he put on 177 at about 4.5 runs an over with Geraint Jones – their fourth century stand in 19 matches together. "We have a great relationship on and off the field and enjoy batting together," said Flintoff. "Our games are worlds apart and that probably makes things more difficult for the bowlers."

After 12 overs with the second new ball, there was not even a slip in. Flintoff was eventually lbw to Australia's new quickie Shaun Tait for 102 and England went on to post their highest first-innings score of the series. Flintoff was so pleased he went back to the hotel that night and danced a little jig of happiness in his room. Especially with Australia quivering at 99 for five at the close. Flintoff put Elton John's "Rocket Man" on in the dressing room and played it, very loudly, again, and again and again.

After Flintoff dismissed Gilchrist the next day, thanks to the catch of the series from Andrew Strauss at third slip, Australia crumbled. And followed on – yes, followed on, for the first time in 17 years.

It was harder for England's bowlers the second time. Simon Jones, who had taken five wickets in the first innings, was out of the game with an ankle injury so bad that it ruled him out of the last Test and the winter tour of Pakistan. And Flintoff was struggling with ankle problems of his own. But the yeomen flogged themselves at the Nottinghamshire ground and, despite contributions from most of the Australian middle order, England needed only 129 for victory. Trescothick and Strauss made a steady start and, after a quiver, things were suddenly comfortable at 103 for five with Pietersen and Flintoff in. They then became sheer panic at 116 for seven with Ashley Giles and Matthew Hoggard in against an unplayable Shane Warne and a pumped-up Brett Lee.

"The pressure and tension in the dressing room was unbelievable," wrote Flintoff for his column in *The Sun*. "All common sense had left me and I had feelings I have never experienced before and never want to have again. I thought I was going to be sick."

But Hoggard and Giles, somehow without panic, got them through. Hoggard, a batsman infamous for his lack of flourish with the bat, somehow produced a cover drive that was a thing of beauty and took England to within four of the target. Giles did the rest.

After the game, the Australians came to England's dressing room for a drink. There were no bottle-openers, so Flintoff put the cold bottles in his jaw and ripped the tops off with his teeth. For the third Test in a row, the players were mingling after the game – a ritual many thought had left the game forever. "Sharing a drink together is not something players from England and Australia have done for a long time and I think we've gained their respect because of it," said Flintoff. "We've learnt things too. You can't help but learn when you chat to the best side in the world."

The series was not only redefining cricket, it was also representing all that is great about true sporting contests. And there was still one match to go. England were 2–1 up, but Australia only had to draw the series to retain the Ashes. The country had gone Ashes bonkers. Even television companies in Japan and Norway negotiated deals to cover the Oval Test. Flintoff, Giles, Harmison, Hoggard and Jimmy Anderson were roped in to promote the government's eat five pieces of fruit and vegetables a day campaign. This was an interesting new venture for Flintoff, a man who had earlier in the year admitted that he drank 24 units of alcohol a week and that his favourite snack was fish fingers, beans, chips and bread. A fourth cousin of Flintoff's was dug up to write a column for a Sunday newspaper and Rachael Flintoff was revealed as one of the faces of the National Lottery. Ian Botham announced that "win or lose the Ashes I'm going to find the best bottle of red wine in town and present him [Flintoff] with it". Oval tickets were the most sought-after commodity around.

It was another knuckle-grinder, another epic. That the game, the series, the Ashes was still in

Left: A cool head was required as England started the fifth Test at the Oval on 8 September 2005 needing just a draw to regain those elusive Ashes.

doubt at lunch on the final day of the final Test had been inconceivable when the Australians arrived just three months earlier. But it was – and it was only with each passing wicket-less over on the last afternoon, that England truly believed they had done it. In the end, there was a slight anti-climax as the game was eventually called off by the umpires simultaneously picking up the bails from the middle during a pitch inspection. But at last, to England, the spoils.

Shane Warne dominated the Test, his last in England, taking 12 wickets in the match to bring his total for the series to 40. But unlike in previous years, when just a look and a roll of the wrist from Warne was enough to bring England to their knees, this time they coped – and got runs from the other end – managing 377 in their first innings thanks to a hundred from Strauss and another mature innings from Flintoff, this time of 72.

The Australian openers came good at last, both getting centuries, but they were thwarted by the weather and England kept the faith. Flintoff, who on the fourth day bowled 14.2 deadly quick overs unchanged from the Pavilion End, was supreme. He picked up his first five-wicket haul against Australia and considered it to be "one of my finest performances with the ball for England." With Matthew Hoggard also swinging the ball all over the place, England dismissed Australia, who were forced to keep up a frenetic pace in difficult conditions, six short of their own total. England were 34 for one at the close of the penultimate day, but Warne was weaving magic.

When the next day Christopher Martin-Jenkins switched on the *Test Match Special* computer, 18,543 unread messages blinked back at him. It seemed people were pretty excited. Could the Ashes really be 12 hours away from the country's grasp? Hearts sank into chests and chests into knees the next morning when Flintoff was caught and bowled by Warne for eight and England were for 126 for five. But then came Pietersen with the innings of his life. Vaughan later said that he had "something of the genius in him" and it certainly seemed that way as Brett Lee's last-ditch three

overs after lunch went for 37 runs and Pietersen's back-against-the-wall stand finished with him hitting fifteen fours and seven sixes in his 158. By the time he was out at five o'clock, England were safe and it was all over bar the formalities.

England did a victory lap of the manic Oval. They looked unbelieving, relieved, thrilled, exhausted. Flintoff admitted to having tears in his eyes. "We had tried our guts out for the past ten weeks, we had the Ashes in our hands and we could see what it meant to everyone," he said.

He was England's Man of the Series (Warne was Australia's) and won the inaugural Compton-Miller medal, named after two great Ashes heroes of the past. The 194 overs he bowled in total were surpassed by no other Englishman and only by Warne overall. He finished the leading English wicket taker with 24 wickets at 27.29 and 18 of his victims were top-seven batsmen. He scored 402 runs at 40.20 – only Trescothick and Pietersen scored more. And no-one scored more quickly or, Lee apart, bowled faster. "It would be nice if we could find an Andrew Flintoff somewhere," said Ponting afterwards. "I'm sure we'll be looking as soon as we get home."

The Australian and English players sat together in the dressing rooms drinking and chewing the fat after the presentations were over before heading off into a very long night. For Flintoff the celebrations were just beginning.

A few days later it was announced that he and Rachael were expecting a second child. He might end up naming a generation – Freddie was expected to rocket up the chart of most popular boys' names. He won the PCA Player of the Year award for the second year in a row.

Flintoff's autobiography was on the shelves by the beginning of October. He and Rachael and Holly did a spread in *Hello!* magazine (Kevin Pietersen and his mum were one of the other celebrity couples featured). He moved house, from his Cheshire cottage to a three-storey, five-bedroomed Georgian house in a gated development, in footballer land.

Companies queued up to sponsor him. This year his earnings from sponsorship were estimated at

Right: Rachael Flintoff and baby Holly celebrate with the other players' families as England clinch a 2–1 series win over Australia.

£1 million – from Barclays, *The Sun*, Volkswagen, Red Bull, Thwaites and Woodworm. His Lancashire benefit in 2006 is expected to be record-breaking. Max Clifford, the publicist, guessed that Flintoff, with his good-bloke image, could earn up to £5 million in the next year if he wanted to – though the guess is that Flintoff would not want the exposure for him or his family. "I just want a quiet life when I'm away from the cricket," he said before the series started. But that quiet life is going to get more and more difficult to keep a grip on. His every move will come under intensive scrutiny and with the adulation will come the desire, by some, to knock him down.

For now, though, he is adored by the young and old, men and women. For his genuineness, his kindness, his contrary traits of the ordinary and the superhuman. As Peter Roebuck wrote: "An ancient craving had been fulfilled. Another Lancelot had been found."

His heroics transcended sport – putting him on the front page – and he was favourably compared to footballers like Wayne Rooney, for whom money and fame has come without responsibility. Flintoff is generous to a fault, uncomplicated. He cares little for image – he used to get his hair cut in the Old Trafford dressing room. He cares not for which bat he uses – any will do. He seems to have no desire for the celebrity life.

"He still goes out drinking with his old mates, never forgets where he came from and no matter what anyone tells him to do you will never get him to live on lettuce leaves and be in bed by 9pm," Stuart Law told *The Sun*.

He flew across the world to play for the World XI against Australia in the Super Series ("I just don't see myself as one of them – it's like I'm the mascot or something") and was mobbed. When he arrived in Melbourne on an early flight with Rahul Dravid, India's galactic batsman, Dravid was snubbed and Flintoff courted by the media. He got a standing ovation in his duties as a drinks waiter during a World XI warm-up match. And at a function in Melbourne, a female fan wore a Flintoff mask with "God" written over the face.

The obsession has hit the sub-continent, too. "India has been hankering after an all-rounder ever since Kapil Dev quit," says Sharda Ugra of *India Today*, South Asia's most widely read news weekly. "And as Flintoff munched his way through the Ashes, India felt that absence more keenly. Whenever he turned up you knew things would happen; if an Australian partnership was growing, you knew wickets would fall, if he was batting, you knew the pressure on the England line-up would ease. His presence literally grew during the series and you got a feeling that England's bowling attack was led by him, and in the end that England were led by him.

"He seems to have figured how and where to use and how to balance aggression – I don't think he's going to be ripping off too many shirts now. He doesn't have a nasty edge to him, and he seems to have figured out where cricket and aggression is in perspective to life at large. He's sort of what the Aussie team would be without their travelling mental-disintegration-psychological-warfare-trash-talk-media-campaign nonsense."

Even the Spanish got in on the act. "La llegada de Flintoff representa un regreso a las valores tradicionales ingleses: es decir, el borracho bonachon, el soldado libertino, como ejemplo a seguir" wrote a Spanish newspaper, which the *GuardianUnlimited* website translated as: "The arrival of Flintoff represents a return to traditional English values: the genial drunk, the libertine soldier, as an example to follow."

Opportunity seems to stretch out endlessly before him. "He's at his physical peak," his physio Dave Roberts has said, "and will retain that level for another two or three years."

Ahead of him, in the winter of 2005–06, Flintoff had tours to Pakistan and India, with Sri Lanka and Pakistan coming to England the following summer. Then, in December 2006, England will attempt to retain the Ashes and, in 2007, win the World Cup. He wants to captain England one day. It seems very probable. The world is at his feet.

Not bad for a fat lad ... except, of course, he isn't anymore.

Previous pages: Steve Harmison gets his hands on the famous urn, Freddie gets his hands on the first of many beers; Left: This is what it feels like to win the Ashes.

THE STORY SO FAR...

Full name Andrew "Freddie" Flintoff
Born 6 December 1977, Preston, Lancashire
Batting style Right-hand bat
Bowling style Right-arm fast
Major teams Lancashire, England, ICC World XI

INDIVIDUAL HONOURS

Professional Cricketers' Association Young Player Of The Year 1998
Cricket Writers' Club Young Player Of The Year 1998
Wisden Cricketer of the Year 2004
ICC One-Day Player of the Year 2004
Professional Cricketers' Association Player of the Year 2004 & 2005
Inaugural Compton-Miller Medal winner 2005
ICC Joint Player of the Year 2005 (with Jacques Kallis)

TEST RECORD
Statistics in brackets show Flintoff's figures since July 2003

Test debut	England v South Africa at Nottingham, 23–27 July 1998
Matches	52 (31)

Batting

Runs	2641 (1998)
Highest score	167 (167)
Average	33.43 (43.43)
Centuries	5 (4)
Half-centuries	17 (15)

Bowling & fielding

Wickets	143 (110)
Average	32.31 (27.86)
Five-wkt innings	2 (2)
Best bowling	5–58 (5–58)
Catches	34 (20)

ONE-DAY INTERNATIONAL RECORD
Statistics in brackets show Flintoff's figures since June 2003

ODI debut	England v Pakistan at Sharjah, 7 April 1999
Matches	90 (38)

Batting

Runs	2313 (1294)
Highest score	123 (123)
Average	34.52 (49.76)
Centuries	3 (3)
Half-centuries	14 (8)

Bowling

Wickets	96 (52)
Average	24.56 (21.05)
Five-wkt Innings	0 (0)
Best bowling	4–14 (4–14)
Catches	29 (10)

All statistics correct as at 1 October 2005